CANADA

John Hartley Williams was born in Cheshire and grew up in North London. He was educated at William Ellis School, and at the universities of Nottingham and London. He now teaches English at the Free University of Berlin, where he has been since 1976. He has also lived and worked in France, Francophone Africa and Yugoslavia.

His first book, *Hidden Identities*, was published by Chatto in 1982. He won first prize in the Arvon International Poetry Competition in 1983 with 'Ephraim Destiny's Perfectly Utter Darkness', the centrepiece of his maverick second collection *Bright River Yonder*, a baroque Wild West poetry adventure published by Bloodaxe in 1987 (and a Poetry Book Society Recommendation). Bloodaxe have also published his later collections *Cornerless People* (1990), *Double* (1994), and *Canada* (1997). *Ignoble Sentiments*, a prose memoir (factual) doubled up with a narrative poem (fictional), was published by Arc in 1995.

He has organised poetry readings by visiting poets in Berlin, has promoted poetry workshops there, and was chief perpetrator of two Bloodaxe poetry festivals in Berlin in 1989 and 1992. He has also collaborated on several projects with Matthew Sweeney, including their handbook *Teach Yourself Writing Poetry* (Hodder & Stoughton, 1997). He is co-translator (with Ioana Russell-Gebbett) of Marin Sorescu's *Censored Poems* (Bloodaxe Books, 1998).

JOHN HARTLEY WILLIAMS

CANADA

BLOODAXE BOOKS

ISBN: 1 85224 431 3

First published 1997 by
Bloodaxe Books Ltd,
P.O. Box 1SN,
Newcastle upon Tyne NE99 1SN.

Bloodaxe Books Ltd acknowledges
the financial assistance of Northern Arts.

Cover printing by J. Thomson Colour Printers Ltd, Glasgow.

Printed in Great Britain by
Cromwell Press Ltd, Broughton Gifford, Melksham, Wiltshire.

Canada canada
mon petit canada

— BENJAMIN PÉRET

Acknowledgements

Acknowledgements are due to the editors of the following publications in which some of these poems first appeared: *Angel Exhaust, Bridport Prize Anthology* (1996), *British Council New Writing 6* (Vintage, 1997), *Dog, Poetry Review, Ramraid Extraordinaire, Turret Bookshop Broadsheet* (Bernard Stone & Raymond Danowski), *Upstart, What Poets Eat* (Foolscap, 1994) and *The Wide Skirt.*

Contents

Book Three

BEAN SOUP

Prague

(for Matthew Sweeney)

At the expensive hotel,
festoons of creeper cannot disguise
heartlessness. The tour guide
smiles a warning,

& the taxi-driver asks you:
How much you cost?
What is the total sum of yrself?
He shakes with actuarial laughter.

Take me to Kafka, you instruct.
He shrugs. In a restaurant
are two policemen facing each other,
like chessmen unable to open.

Prague by night, he says.
There's a wink in everyone's eye,
but you they do not desire.
Everybody's middle name is Trotsky.

After supper, yr waiter
rips up the magazine *Elegance*
into bank note sized pieces
& offers it to you as change.

You go to the bar.
A slender unshaven person
slides onto the stool next to you.
He has prominent ears & an anxious smile.

He tells you that language
is no barrier
to the expression of reluctance.
Dare you converse?

Probably not, says the person.
Have you, in life, an ingenious father
who is trying to avoid
using yr real name?

Reveal it to me.
Please. And he leads you out
down narrow streets,
where buildings shape the sky.

Notice, he says, how the city
is marked out in squares.
Let us therefore approach it
knightwise.

You do so. It is a kind
of dance that
has in the execution of
its step a failed feeling.

I am always late, he says.
Punctuality is a knife at my throat.
I have missed my plane, you say.
Leave now, he says.

You have spent no money.
You have seen no sights.
Back at the hotel, the tour hostess
has left a recriminatory note on yr pillow.

You depart, chastened, for the airport.
Moonlight & shadow
determine the moves of yr taxi.
From the glassware shops

decanters wink at you.
A saleswoman is studying a blank cheque.
In a pattern of windows, slowly,
security mesh descends...

Bean Soup

Steve played saxophone like Sonny Rollins
in a cellar in Novi Sad. He had a crazy drummer
from Budapest. An audience of
Tibor, Branko & me.

That was the year
modern jazz came to the Vojvodina,
Steve & I waltzing the Danube
out towards *Ribarsko Ostrvo,*

me blipping the bass line with my lips
& him doodling the tenor solo with his,
smoking a little
of Mike's home grown.

The Danube froze over. It was serious
gloves, hats & coats. That was when I learned to love
winter garments. Nobody really believed in wrapping up warm
where I came from.

We tramped thru birch trees to a cabin,
kicking the snow high.
When we opened the door
the corpse of cigarettes, wild music & brandy fell out.

We reeled back, put our heads down
& went in. 'Bean soup,' said Steve.
We breathed pure garlic farts
& smoke from the charcoal grill.

They brought it in a tureen
full of gypsy gold teeth, smiling up at us.
The beans were hopping
to the pizzicato rhythms of a mad orchestra,

to a melody that danced them
deep into the soulful thighs of the ham,
a spice barrel full of paprika, which went
ba-boom! when we dunked kettledrums of bread in it.

Ribarsko Ostrvo: Fisherman's Island

15

We slurped the fiercest bits. It was
the choicest liquid ever tasted, & it had chosen us.
Our ears prickled to jagged *kolo* music,
the wheel dance, so many little feet this way & that

like beans you can't get on yr spoon, so fast they jiggle,
that way & this. 'How many bean languages can you eat?'
asked Steve. 'Serbian? Hungarian? Danubian?'
The white wine sank a shaft of bliss into our smoky heads

& the table cloth became
a funlovers' guide to the red light district
in agricultural Sremska Mitrovica –
every pig sty a brothel.

We were ignored, except
by the band. They were waiting for us to get drunk.
We drank mulberry brandy, swopped a joint,
& ascended to the right hand of King Bean.

That was the moment the gypsies sneaked up on us,
pulled the corks of our ears with violinistical
twists & turns, loosened off our knees
with a throb-thrum of guitar chords,

planged the shoestrings of our hearts
with voices that wailed on quarter-tones,
till we broke glasses & plates, linked arms,
& danced on the shards.

More drinks. More snow. More cigarettes.
The word for beans in Serbian is *pasulj*, which
made me think of big, wild, white, leaping pussycats.
We put on our fur hats & toppled out the door.

Steve played *Pick Yourself Up.*
I plucked & punched my old violincello.
We cackled & crooned to the crows.
We felt as if we'd eaten the entire fidgety

cloud symphony of the Pannonian plain.
Big black birds were jitterbugging on the boughs
of the sad, silent birch trees. And we cd see
the keeled over masts of sunken wrecks

in the iced-up harbour. We exchanged,
the finest, the sublimest thoughts about life, love
& the best way not to get caught. And later,
when Steve sawed off a finger from his playing hand

in a carpenter's workshop in Hamburg,
& I stopped listening much to Sonny,
& the town grew smaller & paler in my memory,
& much later still, war broke out –

I cd still taste the savage heat of that bean soup,
hear the rhythm of those clenched hambones
beating on the skins of the innocent poor,
taste the mouth lash of that piquant sausage

& see the steam from a single locomotive,
a line of wagons, at least a mile off on the horizon.
Snow's forecast today, coming out of the east, from Russia,
snow whose icy stings drench my face, as I

take my Sunday walk, flicking toefulls of it high.
Each blast of it seems to open that door we crashed out of,
the gypsy band kicking us up the behind,
sending us *Oo Bop Sha Bam* upon our way.

The Knowledge

'Everybody loves somebody sometime...'
DEAN MARTIN

The city plan I carry in my head
thru foggy November boulevards,
over *Grosser Stern* & left into *Mehringdamm*,
is drunken expertise, like
driving too fast, & maybe (dangerous this)
the beginnings of an amorousness...
My passenger leaves quickly, nervous,
at having asked me for a lift.

I drive on thinking of those black & white
B-movies of the fifties, the Korean war,
side by side with Dean Martin & Jerry Lewis,
in colour. Then a statue reminds me
of an earlier war – men hurling Mills bombs, trampling
alphabetic names into a plinth.
No police controls tonight. I'm home
to catch the double feature's better half.

I lift a Cinemascope pan of rich
red bean soup onto the stove, wait for it
to bubble, smell the garlic, then dip
the spoon, feel the bite of hot paprika rise.
If a crazy Asiatic leapt into my foxhole now,
I'd grin & offer him the ladle. Slowly,
those knots of corners untie, round
which I travelled too fast, headlights blazing.

Everyone's asleep, & no recriminations.
This evening someone told me his father died
out there. An Englishman. And the next table
burst into laughter. I thought:
cut the comedy, he was only twenty-one.
Three more glasses of *Königsberger Pils*!
I brood on death. Obliteration. Smoky liquid.
What was he doing in Korea, anyway?

Round the concrete feather that remembers
how the air-bridge kept this city going,
we swerved on home, every corner marked
with what had happened there. *Déjà vu* geography –
a pale paperchase thru the weightless past.
Against the VistaVision whiteness of the streets,
I saw in the reflecting windscreen's glow
a face averted from the spectre of a kiss.

I sensed her worried nearness, her
posture measuring our anxious forwardness.
There was a cool, erotic shadow in the air...
'Here!' she said. I pulled up hard against
the kerb. She glanced once, then left
the stale, smoke-upholstered snakepit of my car.
I drove away. My foglamp beams picked out
a forage chain of joined pedestrians.

Now the bean pot's open. Steam heals.
I suck the bone that gives me back the marrow –
the tinkle of her keys, like a dog tag, falling,
warmth in the kitchen, the technicolour thought
that it was Dean who always got the girl.
On windswept corners stand policemen, waiting...
In my eyes' mirror, I can see lovers
slipping my embrace like indifferent ghosts.

Pyjama Story

I woke in the night —
my sweat-stressed pyjamas were devouring me.
Three shades of blue stripes
that worked on me toothlessly.

Urgently, I had to leave for Vietnam.
There I met a girl, but her plump sister
had me in the paddy-field.
Was it my imperial nightwear?

It wasn't her, but the thin one
I wanted. The fat sister
cd easily become China.
I'd stand accused of deviation.

Portly, she put me between her legs
with the gravity of a dictator.
Her sister & the villagers were watching.
Cream Lusty had thighs like horses.

You'll get pyjamas, I said,
all of you, real sleep garments,
I promise you.
Then we emigrated to Britain.

In the shop, our sole recreation was reading
noodle packets from Japan.
I felt like the Mikado, with a sister on each arm.
I explained our customs.

See little Jesus, on that shelf up there, I said.
We gazed & he peed tenderly into our mouths.
It's the English equivalent of sake, I said.
Wraith Fire giggled like a mountain spring.

Behind the bead curtain of our establishment,
the machines were sewing pyjamas,
merrily ticking clocks of speeded up time,
whizzing thru nights & days,

unpicking the fabric of society.
The authorities questioned me.
Is this a marriage of convenience?
What are all these sewing machines for?

Why is it so steamy & warm in here?
Who are these semi-nude fat men,
fanning each other with strips off the Union Jack?
Are you married to both these women?

I croaked my excuses.
What the girls seemed to be offering, they weren't.
They did things differently in Asia.
It was a race against time to provide people with pyjamas.

Wraith Fire touched me with fine fingers.
In my crazy night suit, I was just
another deluded citizen, trying to do good, creeping
uselessly over borders that were closed.

They asked for birth certificates –
Nothing recent, I said. They yanked my fashion-
ably pointed beard. I folded my capacious sleeves,
bowed & pointed to Wraith Fire.

This is the woman I really love, I said,
We cannot allow her villagers to sleep nude at night.
They sneered & reached into their waistbands.
Using oriental knives, they slashed my pyjamas to rags.

Christmas in Paris

Joggers rose from the fountain.
Their bronze trainers
were stained with centuries
of standing still.

Suddenly the tape-reindeer
were switched on. Those blunted hooves.
The treeless lanes
of *St Sulpice* were cold.

From under a grating
I heard a sinister music.
Policemen were dancing
to an ancient tune.

I crossed the city,
entered *Samaritaine*,
& wandered
its dusty floorboards.

Two Algerians were prowling
with a girl they called Sylvie.
They winked at me thru spokes,
discussing pedals, gears, chains.

From that high window
in the cycle department,
I saw their spaceship
had not yet lifted off.

It was gathering
silent vacationers
in the rim of its great exhaust.
I hurried from the store,

half-expecting to hear
the roar of unspeakable engines.
The girls wore anoraks & glances.
The lights were coming on.

Over *Pont Neuf*, up *St Michel*...
thru looming iron gates, I entered
the ghostliness
of the *Jardin du Luxembourg* at dusk.

Sylvie sat by the pool.
She touched a crystal finger to her lips,
let fall a book of poems
into the reflecting water: *splash.*

I read her caution & nodded.
The man with a cart of model boats
had loaded up & was pushing for home.
Back on the street again,

a horse reared above traffic.
Its stone rider threw up a hand.
I thought of her sitting there alone.
Too late now to change my plans.

What had happened to her companions?
From under the street,
came louder music. Heavier dancing.
I tried to interpret the cries.

It was unmistakable:
the lurching rhythm of the stamping feet,
the knocked-over chair,
the shouting...

Night fell. I saw the *bateaux mouches*
sailing to the liberty statue
up the darkened river. I saw faces,
white behind smoked glass.

Was that Sylvie, I thought,
performing a foolish pavane
in the shadow of an empty building,
dancing alone, or for the unblinking stars?

A Word from Istvan Kovács

(for Ken Smith)

Adjusting the string of my hat,
chin propped on my brass-capped stick,
I survey my pigs with a windmill eye.
When the well-pole tilts, it draws thousand year old water
from the river of my race.

Potatoes this year will be red & crisp,
fleshy to the teeth like a well-planned crime.
Peppers will be yellow & heavy,
sit in the hand like a judge's mace,
weigh down yr palm with verdicts.

I came here, you understand, with Genghis Khan
to destroy Christendom. Well, well, I thought.
You can imagine my surprise when I planted
cucumbers, beans, cauliflowers,
& they came up Christian as a girlfriend.

On a three-legged stool, by a basket of geraniums,
I wear a cloak & a woven shirt. Sunday best.
The golden clasp of my cloak is hot in the sun.
It matches the glint of my buckle.
Soon, I know, the people will come.

The donkeys put on an act of hilarity.
My cart-horse, still in the shafts, rubs its back
against a tree, tipping a wheel off the ground.
The land is flat as the vowel I use
to gee them up along the tufty track.

I see them from far off. A car across the plain.
On the high banks of the river, the trees bend & hiss.
The sky is tuned to a low resonance of wind,
like a rumour of those who resisted, the ones
who were taken away, the non-returnees.

When the guests arrive, I tip the demijohn
against my shoulder. Their eyes watch
the way it floods out – greeny-gold *kövidinka*
from the last barrel. What hospitality means
is showing the plenty you'd like to have.

I raise my glass in a cracked toast, & they try,
fumbling with the language, to repeat it.
Waiting for food, I become impatient,
let out the old familial roar of my blood
that sends the women flying into the kitchen.

'Where are you from?' I ask, imagining it,
as the women serve & retreat. The new
visitors come from the west. They praise
my viticulture. Slowly, I take my hat off
& they stare at the whiteness of my brow.

Onions might be the text for a sermon.
Garlic, the hard, white giver, its tang
richer, more forceful than a young boy's jet
might scandalise our barns this Autumn.
Shallots, I murmur, are thicker-skinned than that.

My gap-toothed grin. *Erös kolbász*,
'Here,' I say, pushing smoked pork fat
across the table, 'you never tasted anything
like this.' I think of it sclerosing their insides
like rust on an ancient drum. I think of them

back in their own country, the futtering vitriol
slowing them, winding them down,
becoming a stone in their stomachs.
Low in the trees, from the banks of the river,
the sun chips at the quartz of my buckle.

Erös kolbász: spicy sausage

25

Mary of Memory

I climbed the cobbled street
of an Italian town,
& stopped to look inside
the window of a shop.

Beyond the farm produce
I saw quite distinctly
the madonna herself, with long black hair,
the keeper of cheeses.

I went into the cool dark.
On the tiled floor a boy squatted
with a dog between his knees,
trying out his conversation.

When I went out again, I felt the heat.
Walking the ramparts, I saw in the vegetable plot below
sunflower hearts turning black
under the fulminating sky.

The corded trunks
of the olive trees
were like nude grandparents,
wrestling...

I cd see country roads
criss-crossing the plain beneath
between the vineyards & the barns,
a map of Lilliput...

Her image came back to me, later.
I was decanting
olive oil thru a funnel
into a curved, tan bottle.

Watching its loquacious
gulps, I felt like that boy,
resentful at speech's difficulty.
Across the flagged sill,

a doorframe rasped
& my older self stepped in –
with a ready wit, of course –
& stood sniffing the cowbreath aroma.

26

She smiled, questioningly.
My younger self stroked the silk ear
of the dog. The adult man
made a joke about the extra virgin cold-

pressed liquid in
the canisters too high to reach,
& gazed at her slenderness as
she turned & stretched up.

My younger self
murmured to his dog. He cd feel
the warm shudder of its flanks.
He knew what an interloper I was.

The stranger's words
were coarsened with use.
He laid his money on the counter.
He looked down at the boy.

It wd be useless to explain
about *ampullae*, Graeco-Roman,
recovered from the ocean bed,
in which a thin crust

is all that remains of the oil,
how that edible wafer dissolves on the tongue,
chilling & slaking the mouth
with its horny taste.

King Lear at the Open Air Theatre, Minack, Cornwall, in 1964

The proscenium was Atlantis,
& Cordelia was upset. Liz,
            of the unlimited cigarettes
& the club foot, dress riding her stocking's hem,
calmed the director, self-possessed.

During rehearsal, she smoked
on the warm steps & kept
            an eye on the breakers,
prompting Lear, who was
always rewriting the script.

Mornings, the cast ate mackerel, wavy
cross marks over limpid green,
            sixpence from a bucket,
a taste that comes back out of memory
like water darkening sunlit stone.

First night, & a storm came
pat for Shakespeare's.
            The audience strained
to follow words against the wind, which
weren't the playwright's, but Lear's.

Iambic pentameters. The stage-prop
thunder mimicked heavenly dynamite.
            There was a sheer drop.
The drenched actors
confused stage left with stage fright.

Liz found a hobo lover.
Cordelia threatened to leave.
            Goneril & Reagan smirked.
The girls' caravan had rocked all night.
Liz was banished to the beach.

The costume mistress was in love
with someone who was only willing to oblige.
            The stage manager was queer.
The director walked a strand of pebbles, plotting...
The King of France had the only car.

Nights, the spot came up anyway,
& Brother Tim climbed out upon a rock,
           forcing three notes from a bugle.
He was giving up the cloth for a woman.
Out there in darkness, he wobbled as he blew

& everybody held their breath. The sea
rolled against the skirts of the cliff.
           As the sennet sounded,
the audience made a gale of its appreciation,
which the wind carried off in a huff.

Behind that embattled comedy
you sensed other lost productions
           rising from the waves,
drained of colour, as if another world
had mounted a pale counterattraction.

Kings, slender & white.
Queens, low-voiced & unchaste.
           Costumes sewn
by the crab-seamstress herself.
The gala heralded by a conchblast.

Nevertheless, at evenings & matinees,
Tim's brassy flourish still rose into the air,
           a fluffed triplet.
It hung out its unsteady phrase,
like an emblem of the divided kingdom.

The Court of Atlantis shimmered
thru the heat of endless summer.
           Recalling, later, that July,
it seemed flawed, somehow – as if trails
of sirrus had spoiled a perfect Cornish sky.

It left a recollection, sharp as a blade.
Impossible to forget those moments,
           when Liz dozed off & Lear dried,
& the silence split open. The watchers beheld
a naked Queen rising from the waves,

whipping the turtles that drew her barque.
On the stage's frozen semicircle,
           Lear looked like a man
beyond surprise or sixpence, his arms raised,
jutting the beard that had got him the part.

Was it the unconscious of the actors
summoning highly-sexed players
                    to voice oceanic thoughts?
What was the audience looking at,
as they collected their things & rose in tiers,

hand at their open throats, to stand a moment,
gazing out across the blinded sea
                    in which the sun's ball had doused?
Was there a hairline crack in the glass
of the evening? Something else to see?

The play finished. There were other things to do.
Taxis came to the field, the caravans rocked
                    one last time maybe. And the Minack
theatre went quiet. The weather wrote its review.
But a voice said: bring back the lights.

Bring back the costumes, the scribbles
on programmes, kisses tasting of sleep.
                    Bring back The Fool, jobless & dripping.
Haul him up from the deep.
He shd have died hereafter.

Bring back the first night nerves & the sun
turning the sea blank as it fell in,
                    & a heart-skipping peal on the horn
launched the play into something you couldn't stop.
Bring back the applause.

The Breakfast

He goes down the street, opens the door.
A big fan swats the pan-smoke.
Crude white neon illuminates the eggs.
Have those burgers been on the flame-grill for years?
The sexy waitress is taking an order
as she wd for anybody, nobody.

He scratches back a chair. Nobody
has told them about that flapping door
thru which, as he sits, she yells the order –
beans, flavoured with the usual smoke,
regular teamugs, flooded for years,
the glibbery sunshine of same old eggs.

She swaggers back with a dish of eggs.
Those too-tight jeans are a come-on to nobody.
She's been teasing her customers for years,
that beyond the mysterious kitchen door
is a place of great femininity & smoke,
where chaos declines into religious order.

But that's all. The special order
will take a while. Not the sizzle of eggs,
he thinks, nor appetising bacon smoke
can make his hunger wait. Nobody
really knows what's simmering beyond the door.
It's everything he's missed in years.

He drags a cigarette. The hit takes years.
He'll know it, when it comes, that order –
someone simply walking thru a door
holding a plate with two hearts-of-yolk eggs,
setting them down as if she was nobody,
meeting his eyes with a gaze of smoke.

The special, all right. He puffs the smoke
away from her face, unkissed for years,
& holds her trembling waist. 'Nobody,'
he whispers, letting his hands slide high, 'can order
me not to do this,' & cups the tender eggs
of her breasts. It's open wide. The door.

Smoke engulfs them, & the order.
Cracking like eggs, the years fall open.
He walks with nobody thru that door.

31

On Vauxhall Station, I Think of Shirts

A slowtrain comes. Doors stand open
to the light. Beneath a poster
                    of a man in mirror sunglasses,
(bare to his waist), the platform
is an ironing board.

The train is an iron.
Life is a shirt.
           What follows
are my weird rules
for pressing:

1. If you're not the signal, you're
                         reading it.
2. Do not stand too close to the edge.
3. Do not stand too far away.
4. Continue reading.

The man in bluejeans
assaults me with his
              homo-erotic leer.
He's beginning to lose face.
Pollution is scrubbing him out.

In the stopped train
are men in suits, England's virtues,
                 with crooked elbows
to hang umbrellas in. They do
the crossword with a straight pen.

At fifty, they've learned
to enjoy the silent maracas
                of their bones,
how to dance
the hush-hush skeleton tango.

If this train started,
& scandal jolted her leg
               against them,
over points, & she
brushed closer, whispering

in the entrance
to a tunnel, that moment when,
                    the lights gone out,
a shock pitched her to them,
soft as a thought, they'd get the clue.

But they wouldn't show it.
The train hums quietly to itself,
                    then leaves.
I do a step from side to side
in the patient shuffle of waiting.

I think
of a woman in a shirt-shop
                    fingering someone's neck
as if it were marble, smiling
blindly into the face of a customer.

The unworn shirts
of the dead rustle
                    under cellophane,
a kaleidoscope of stripes
that shiver & seethe.

Then loudspeakers rip open
the quiet packet of the air,
                    names pulled out like electric pins,
a cackly cascade
of dim destinations –

& far off down the track, another train
comes silent up the line. It isn't going
                    my way, either.
When it's gone, I stretch my arms out wide
& slip into the armholes of the afternoon.

The Novice

I was a merchant in ambrosia.
Bring back, they said, honey from the Andes.
I walked to the airline office
& told them my aim.

Several miles high, I sat
clutching my thoughts.
We landed at a difficult airport.
I took a bus to a village & hired a donkey.

The air was full of warm rain
that couldn't fall. There were
basilicas on the hillside. Then, like sculptures
or fallen rocks, there were the Indians.

I knew the story of their origin.
They were a loving, yet stony-hearted race.
Their coffin faces
betrayed no hint of anything.

On one particular day,
the small, pious children,
attached to a relative by tiny handhold,
were brought to church.

Fettered in the darkness,
they were left
for low-flying Andean bees to ponder.
I had never seen such apian mammoths.

My guides
let me witness the act of sweetness giving.
They showed me where best to hear
the grotesque buzzing, the childish, expiring sighs.

I returned to the city, took to wearing
sunglasses, using the wrong name.
Outside my room at the *Extravagancia*,
barefoot women prowled the corridors.

Nights, there were soft, curious bumpings
on the window-pane. I lay in my own sweat,
rapturous with imagined stings.
My creamcurd language fused with the bees' fury.

At dawn the Indians came. They brought
urns, vases, amphora, calabashes, crocks.
A viscid spate of brilliant stickiness
overflowed everywhere...

When I spoke to them
they smiled like intelligence pegged to the ground
that knows it will be devoured
by something more primal than itself.

Indians remember
what feelings once were.
The loquacity of their silence
is extreme.

Yet they were not averse to gaiety.
Why not summon the ghost of flavour?
Above my head, a giant moth
circled the fly-cemetery of the lamp.

I lay, as they instructed, naked on the bed.
Their tongues worked every pore of my skin
until I bled a fustian syrup.
You too are a hive, they said. And left me.

I lay sleeping at last.
Dreams thumped for entry to my brain.
At the airport, the girl could not understand me.
I opened the cell of her ear with a word.

In the plane I turned out my pockets.
They were full of bee husks.
When the stewardess stooped
towards me, her cheeks flamed with proximity –

it seemed we might crash. Now,
I sit on a pile of baggage, in customs,
a pollen stain disfiguring my smile.
What I have to declare is this.

Morning After

After a good night's sleep,
I woke a new man.
My name was Crenshaw
& I was fat.

In the mirror I saw
the three wounds of love –
meeting, union
& separation.

I wore a cicatrice
curved like a Turkish sword,
one to each cheek
& one on my brow.

I remembered
too much about myself.
The birch trees.
The old house.

I could recall
the three men who came –
Armbutt, Spooker & Lubb.
Their polished sedan

drew to a halt
on my carefully sifted gravel.
I knew once again
the taste of carpet.

When the sun pierced the mist
around eleven o clock,
I saw the church
silent in green.

I saw the vicar, his henhouse eyes,
He'd opened his arms to welcome those
who streamed towards its door
as if toward escape.

Then the mist descended again.
I could hear footsteps
on the tarred road, neither
coming nor going.

And years later,
when everything had faded
in my memory,
I entered my own house,

& lay down on my bed,
closed my eyes
& dreamed that if
I stayed awake

the whole night thru,
I'd be
my old self again
by morning.

The Croak Exposed

I tried to stretch out
Capturing her vessel with my tie

I pulled her towards me
And the next thing I knew

Was the fervent iconoclasm
Of her surrender

It was a bad direction
We were headed for open sea

And out there, I knew
Were deepwater shoals

Of reverential
Nothingness

*

Then we were becalmed
On a windless Sargasso

She whispered to me
In a language of brushstrokes

Weedlike trees raised green umbrellas
Like a glass to silence

Speaking was no more
Than a finger laid across the lips

*

Rescue came...
Bare-chested sailors...

Admiring the wetness of her dress
They brought us to their dismal society

I took her under the lee of my darkness
Showed her the cold

Where the wind gusted between tower blocks
Skinhead bullyboys stopped us

They touched her ankles with tobaccoey fingers
Touched her nipples with silver knives

They waved off our pleas impatiently
Waved off innocence with ring-studded hands

Slashed open the doors of apartments
From bottom to top

And beckoned us to enter
With the viciousness of goodbye

                    *

We took the lift to a room
High above the city

Empty of furniture & memory
A new way of being wrong

I embraced her from behind
My pinions circled her, cupping her breasts

I was a world feather-weight translator
Of the ecstasy into the mud

'Is this what you want?' she asked me fiercely
Questions, solicitations, acquiescence

I was dawn flooding the heart of a postman
I was evening stuck in the throat of a priest

I was the smell of the interior of the police station
In which a dog licks the scuffed shoes of a weeping man

I was the janitor of that unspeakable building
Sweeper of the body's corridors

I was thorns in the crown of her complicity
The croak of causes everywhere

Thru which the chaos is
Uncased, disclosed

The City

We came down thru the forest,
horses delicate across the stones
of a dried stream-bed,
hooves crushing the fallen husks

of pine-cones. So cold it had been,
you'd think winter reinvented
itself to try us. There was
a dry clarity in the air

that made our skin itch
& thinned our hair to thread.
Our lips were scaly with it,
our bones were nearly seized.

We moved with a deliberateness
our bodies cd not hold back.
The ache of our progress
had long stopped talk dead.

Emerging from the sting of branches
onto the plain, we saw
the high walls of a place
we had not seen before, except

we knew it as if we had.
It was utterly distant
yet close
as a weight in our saddlebags.

We went towards it, not knowing
if it were ten miles or a hundred off.
The land showed us
hidden things as we rode past.

A woman on scratched knees
raised her arms. Someone took
a whip to bedraggled children.
From a broken doorway, a mouth opened.

Along the beach of a river
columns of men stooped & swung.
The silence of their buried resistance
was rhythmed with commands.

In a stone-field, great wheels of wood
were raised above the rocks.
Most were still, but a single donkey
obeyed the ghost of an order,

driving our gaze upwards
as men & women
pinned to the spokes
revolved into the cool sky.

On the descent,
they brushed thru flails & knives,
wrapping us
in a thin tissue of faint screams.

I saw that one man,
as the vane lifted him up
& brought him down, had his eyes open
watching us. And when,

idly, one of our men flicked the donkey,
& it broke into a ragged gallop
& the cuts & blows fell faster,
his mouth opened wide

& his face vanished into it, as if
into a pool. We jerked our spurs,
urged our mounts up a slight incline
to the edge of that pitted field.

The city was no nearer.
The sky was stretched upon our gaze,
drumhead tight, its presence
drained of pulsations,

a glintless diamond, with no
colour at its core. It seemed to hold
blue's absence preciously.
The chill that it exuded

(curiously enough)
made us think of a flame
raging somewhere, invisibly
raging, seeking an escape.

We rode on.
Sometimes we passed troops of people –
families they might once have been –
pleading & begging in a language

no one cd really understand. And they,
losing trust in what they found
in their own mouths,
spoke softer & softer, so that

we had to lean down
to catch the breath of their speech,
flake–crystal consonants, drifting vowels,
the kind of snow that never really starts to fall.

The map we followed was in our heads.
It brought us to the ramparts of the city.
We reined in the squadron. Our horses'
nostril smoke feathered the cold.

Something creaked.
We contemplated thick planks,
observed the lurching descent
of a wooden tongue from a stone mouth.

We saw a cobbled street
winding up, & waited,
knowing that smoke from chimneys
had to come from somewhere, that

Cobbler, Hotel,
Saddlery, Ironmonger,
had been written
on buildings by men.

We felt the pull of it.
Chips of earth flew up
where the drawbridge had hit the frozen turf,
& fell back into stillness.

We wanted to cross.
Our horses wanted to cross.
The granite archway beckoned us.
As evening drew near,

the sky was simply a bruise.
Our scoured faces yearned for forwards.
Our horses trod the spot. Our bodies bent from the waist.
Yet still we did not move.

PISTOL SONNETS

BOOK ONE

Our Hero

I speak French without tears
I know the Serbo-Croat for love
I have City & Guilds bomb-laying
Life is simplicity to me

I know an obstacle when I see one
I have ideograms sewn into my underwear
I throw paper aeroplanes at the secretaries
I have mastered the art of fear & trembling

I hear a mewing in the wainscot
I write sonatas for missing pets
I dedicate them to fog, to trams
I drag my girlfriend thru the cemetery by her hair

In the weeds among the fallen tombstones
I make her look at my face: 'There!'

Hello, My Lovely

I was holed up in bed with the dumb blonde Meaning
And a flask of Scotch. In the lamplit street below
Stood a man with a snap-brim mobster's hat
I said: 'You know the way *subjunctives* go...?
It means the way I think of you
Let's underdivide it, anxiety doll
Let's make the doubts we have feel true!'

But they were close
The type that smile before they waste a fellow. Then tap
Cigar ash in his blinded face
I told her to relax
She slipped her nightie off. What a frail!
'Don't worry, sweets,' I said, 'yr sexual identity
Is absolutely safe with me...'

Nothing Like a Good, Old-Fashioned
English Murder Mystery

The novel tells you where the ramblers walked
How they got lost & separated in fog
How each was murdered, impaled on a stile
Felled by a boulder, or back at the YHA
Poisoned with a welcoming cup of Nescafé

But do we, as readers, really care?
Finding out who did it, when they're all dead, anyway
Or not finding the heroine in our bed
Is what happens when you turn to the end first
Nothing of consequence is lost but the middle

But you can't resist it, can you, this turning back?
There she is on page one hundred & one
Someone who knows something you don't, throwing the coverlet back
Smiling like an author, inviting you in

Somewhere on the Polluted Mediterranean

Sonnets are like those old ten inch records
They know in advance
How long to go on, then stop
A fine corrective, madam, to blather

There was a fifteen-year old virgin, alone on the beach
She kept looking at me, till we stole into the pines
A needly path that circled round & round
Away from the sea & the smell of parents
Where two small boats crammed the same harbour
And the holiday gramophone was overwound

This coney reminiscence
Is like the fast hand on a clock
I think we shd stop here & let
Its brevity wait for ever

Lovely, Delicious You

You shook out yr mane & I was adrift
Noticed you did not have the same firm body
Old mechanicals, horsehair sofas looking shoddy
Yr tongue too unwieldy to lift
When I think of you, I think of a river
And a weight that drags on the tide
I think: 'Now how cd I take the strain?'

You need the right tackle for things like this
I fling out a line, & watch the flood take it
In the reel spinning out, I hear yr sigh
I lounge on the bank & pretend to fish
Watching yr curves from a secret angle
And if those little bait hairs don't get tangled
Afternoon Eddy is not my name

Statement

I have a confession to make
I've always loved you & yr bicycle of sadness
Sometimes I did thy laundry   O
I lay with the tearsack between my thighs...
Breakfast, that reflective encounter of used nights...
I put an egg in the window of yr face

Even as you spoke, I got off & pushed
I'm a downhill Girlhood Model in red & green
When I take part in the *Tour de Vagina*
I wrap my missing member in a dishcloth
That's me at the sisterhood end of brotherhood
Our General also likes warm ears & a chat
Do not forsake him, I tell myself
Do not let him cycle off the map

Blue Funk

'Let us suppose, murmured St Augustine
'Like mine, yr baptism were delayed...
When wd you select the propitious moment?
Or is it irony that turns you on?'

'True law confides dissenting paragraphs'
I said pedantically to pleasure's ear

'Aha!' smiled St Augustine. 'Just a contradiction-lover, eh?'
'A shipwreck on a seabed of mistakes...'

And it was true. All across the ocean
Sweet swimmers dived toward my hold
Drummed on my door, soundlessly
Entered the cabin, the bunk I'd occupied so long

Just as I was beginning to enjoy myself
They clanked, naked, against my bones

Roadside Rescue

How ravishing those mechanics are
Who fix yr boulevards at midnight!
They come when they're wanted. They won't leave
Till yr motor's purring in a nightmare

Under their grey, persuasive gaze
Virgins undress for ever
Loose tongued boys become lax & idle
Like canoes in white water, they capsize

They tell you not to leave yr vehicle
They won't go till desire withers
Till an absence of stars has utterly
Blackened this ball you stand on
Till shivering intolerably
You've hung out the 'surrender' sign

The Excuse

I lifted a coffee cup to buildings everywhere
And somewhere in the basement machines
Continued to function...not quite soundlessly...&
Destiny slid a hand toward the switch

There was the swirl of a drink by a spoon
There were the crumbs of bread by a knife
The spider on the kitchen table, old Quick-off-the-mark
And me with my pinching finger, too late

Listen when are you going to fuck me back?
I mean: get the hips of the world into yr thrust?
Do I always have to get you drunk first
Or tell you lies till yr body flows over with passion?

Such solid objects, this board, this chair, this crockery,
                                    these knives & forks
What I want to say next will take a while...

Guest List

Secretaries for bestial dancing
Mermaids in wheelchairs
Bankers with crocodile handkerchiefs
Teachers holding bitten-into apples
Neighbours for noodle salad
Cyclists with one clip too many
Then, of course, the lovers, in bandages
And those truth-soured Judases, the poets

The ear-splitting obviousness of the latter
What makes them think we've not heard it before?
Spouting rhymes as they corner the Queen of Occasion
Savouring each morsel of *thee, thou, thine*...
Slavering with helpfulness, as their hands fumble
Buttons they didn't mean to undo you with...the swine!

Dimanches

The hideous elders are crouching by the fire
They appear to be roasting stinking fish
They're making the usual malodorous distinctions
Each morbillous vowel, a giddy abyss

It's time to take you upstairs
I'm going to read you the riot act
Where do the days go? How can I requite
These obscenities you keep telling me about?

Madonna-face. You
With that shrewd old hag between yr legs

I'm going to set light to the curtains
To the bed-clothes, the wardrobe, the tools of prettification
And then I'm going to be really ugly for you
So we can both go out in a blaze of desire

After Hours

She was struggling with the dress over her head
'Wrong silk!' she cried
She was dark now. Her breasts were teardrops
Her skin rippled & ran
Slowly the rain filled in the blanks
Night music in the feline passageways
The self-wrestling of her body
Sized & stretched like a cool jet of gas
Illuminating the wetness
In the pale glass lantern of an alley
The shantung softness of the evening planet
Thru which a different set of people were going home
Turning out the lamps everywhere
Winding in the awning, stacking up the stars

Love in the Aspect of Neptune

You were cold. Yr knees were chipped
Yr waist was narrow & hard
And my tongue was heavy as a winding sheet
Yr breasts were sodden, you were all tail, like a mermaid
We spoke to each other in fishpouts
Each of our phrases wore a face

What we said lay underneath our saying
Was a wave beneath the surface, the flux
Of a turbulent ocean spring. It was
The deep gargling of a seagod who studied
Wrecks so reflectively
His aahs & umms stirred up tempests
Revealing in the clear mirror of his thought
Cracked-apart vessels, half-open treasure chests
Drowning swimmers with long, beautiful hair...

Everything Was Fine, Until...

You know those fish tanks
They keep in Chinese restaurants
Full of Gladiator Priests, Siamese Ideograms
Finny Kick-Boxers, Mandarin Droolfish?
Did it occur to you that to those impassive guppies
You're the plankton beyond the end of the world
You're the unreachable fronds of Heaven?

Some kind of pond life, anyway
As you forcefeed that girl with crispy-fried noodle
The way she stirs the debris in the bottom of her plate
Do those wavy, plucking movements mean anything?
Are they communication? Or calls for help?
Splashes on yr cheek. Where are they coming from?
What is the mad message of the weeds?

Athens

Rain-streaked Aegean dusk, after dinner
The truth, beautifully unstraight, a Greek utensil
A bare-footed woman crossing the restaurant
A trick of water, the energy of pain

Smell the urgency of the earth
It rises from the warm ground like steam
It's the scribble of heaven since yesterday
Written in the crooked alleys of the dark
With a rustle & a hiss she joins you
Tells you she will leave you. And smiles

Dedicate yr life to no one
The ghost of her departure will be the law
Flesh, sweetness, coldness
Too breathable air beyond the door

Catalpa Tree

Who knows where the roots thrash down to?
Botanists standing here might shiver
Not from the noise of traffic two feet away
But from the deepness of the ground

I remembered you as if it was now
I anticipated yr lecherous smile
You waited for me, the cupboard was dark
We were alone with pullovers

Touch me, you said
I felt you bite off my fingers & nipples
And then yr brown legs cracked the floor
Downward rooting
And the sap of yr sex
Came gushing up thru yr mouth

Pastoral

Even when you're there, I miss you
Yr gold crucifix between yr naked breasts...

I can hear the monks whispering
(Watering the flowers): 'Isn't it about time
We put these monastery beds to rights, Brother Bill?'
'You rake & I"ll pray, Brother Fred.'
'Why don't you do me like you did, Brother Bill?'
'You mow & I'll sow, Brother Fred.'

But when I chase the rabbit out of yr orchard
You cry out

And muttering unfurls beneath our window
As the brethren hold worried conversation:

'Brother Fred, that statue of our saviour...?'

'Oh Lord! Did I do that to his leg?'

R-Evolution

I took off yr panties & celebrated Darwinism
Learned about origins at the point of leaving
My fingers walked the beach of yr ribs
Hand in hand, we went towards the ooze
Our bodies ran backwards, till they became amoeba
Dividing & dividing until they met

We left the room, that bed, that chair
On which our clothes had been so carelessly flung
Lists of things to do slithered out of my pocket
Rolled under the wardrobe, gathering fluff
I wedged an encyclopaedia
Under the waterbed to improve the wallowing
'Don't say "yes"' I said, 'in case it brings back "no"'
We sank unChristianly into the wet

Almost the Finale of the Movie, then This Had to Happen

We've got a chance to reach that crevice, she said
Too late to change the plot now, he said
Without language I couldn't cling here, he said
Fuck language, she said, get me off this cliff

He scrabbled forward & everyone tensed
The rope was fraying on a sharp bit
She looked deeply bored as he started to recite
An incomprehensible poem that wd obviously go on forever

Can't you ever rewrite the script? she said
Smashed his knuckles with a rock & he let go
All the way down he thought of her fondly
It struck him (just before he struck the ground)
That was the rhyme he needed: 'let go'
Before you reach the end & something worse

Naples

Boys whiter than Venus
Girls with thighs like Zeus
The museum is a bedroom
In which marble has fun

It's cool & boring in here
The tourists look sick with innocence
Why are their remarks so
Oracular, sordid & unprepossessing?

O look, dear, this is the Farnese Hercules
Yes, & I'm Jupiter
I'm the filthpot of the planets. Watch me
Sex a nymph's stone crotch with my tongue
And snick the dust from her folds
In lizard-like snatches!

Jungle Drums

No Lana Turner in tight-waisted khaki
To hand him the rifle to plug the wall-eyed buffalo
A wet slap is the map springing back in his face
Stewart Granger will not rescue him now

Then he stumbles on a damp hill
Sweet luggage of memory! It brings back
Melancholy mothers of the moon
Girls who talked endlessly in tents
Porters who played rag time on the portable piano
And the final comeuppance of Dr Abuze, the
Toppled Emperor of Baboof, leaving him
Free to mount the the Throne of Potties, alone

How he ordered the stained suitcase of her body opened
With trembling fingers, unpacked the cool, still-covered bones!

Zeitgeist

Liberty is the bodice of invention
Take it off & show me yr snow-shoulders
Pull my mouth to yr nipples
Freeze me like novocaine
To me you are proof we have evolved
Despite this boring room & the absence of God
Yr ankles rest on twentieth century me
Yr eyes regard me from a ninetenth-century pillow
Needless to say, the dark crux of yr body
Is deep in a pool of middle history
O I wd gladly surrender to you
Now, forever, & retrospectively too
Let the enjoyable chill of you flood my fingers
As a third party climbs the sill

The Devourer

When my love, my patient enemy-licker
Was eaten by a crocodile, I felt sad
All the sperm she had swallowed had turned her sweet
And the reptile recognised that
It knew, instinctively, it seems
What it is about a woman that makes her
So true, so wonderful, so exactly right

My village & my friends were eaten, too
'OK,' I said, 'we'll see about this.' And I went there
Tore the crocodile in pieces & threw it far out to sea
Until it pulled itself together & swam ashore
Having become everybody again
A stern crowd, wading up the beach
Waving bibles & telling me to behave

Let Me Jog You

You were soft as an old sofa. Let the
Skeletal chauffeurs wait with their bony wraps
You were fresh as newly-kneaded dough. Let the
Warmth in my language thaw the winter of time
Let's have some phantom country couplings
Nettle stings on yr behind...strange cool hands on mine...

If I cd remember you, I'd love you more
If I cd hear myself whispering yr name, excitedly
If I cd sink between yr unvisited thighs & hear
Whatever you might have said to urge me on
Couldn't you have left yr bra off that day on the bus?
The past is a cupboard full of unused jam
Couldn't you not have worn yr panties at the circus?
When the trapeze went up, I'd have shared you with everyone!

Epithalamion

Marriage isn't a game of Dracula charades
It isn't swung capes, long fingernails, or always the white shoes
If only those night-revellers wd shut up
You'd think blood thru the ceiling was wonderful
The way they carry on. Johannes & Susanne getting married?
Well, I'm not. No wonder I'm howling at the moon

Wystan Hugh Auden said: *Only marriage is important*
And from that standpoint you can see he was wrong
It doesn't get the teethmarks out of my neck, frankly
Tho I'd like to have a little castle in Transylvania
Be married to both of you, except... Johannes & I
Wd be infamous, Susanne wd sleepwalk in her nightdress...

Look! This is us, cautiously lifting the lid
Risking all, risking nothing. Come...

For Augustine

Time & again I'd like to re-invent
The black vibraharp of yr sweet mouth
The concert grand of yr chuckle
The silence that falls before the applause
I'd like to go back to a tropical downpour
In the African bed of yr tiny room

I'd like to burn with perpetual motion
Constricted & voicey in yr tin chateau
Under yr picture of a radio that really worked
On sheets of satin & plastic that squeaked for hours

I'd like to come home to you
As silly as I went out there
Reminding myself of the time I was skin
When same things wd happen later, too
Completely unknown to us all

The Questions

'S'eu no vos vei, domna, don plus me cal,
negus vezers mo bel pensar no val'

BERNART DE VENTADORN

Wd you sacrifice yr freedom for love?
Have you already done this, without knowing?
To prove yourself worthy of love, wd you
Sacrifice what you have unquestioningly pledged to defend?
Wd you give up yr ambition & content
To experience the full certainty of loving? Wd you do this?
What wd you say to the man who was Judas
If you knew he did it only to please a woman?
Wd you scornfully crush the sluglike advances of life
With the ecstatic foot of admirable love?
If love turned away, how cd she be made to look back?
And were she never seen at all
How wd you recognise the flame's touch?
What cd match yr beautiful thought of her?

Troubadour

Riding the horse thru a meadow of vetch
The ankle of the beast twisted on a rabbit tuft, & I dismounted
Led it downward to a stream
Knelt & fractured my face in silver
With scooping hands, threw back my head
Smelt the clear, sweet air of the *Uzège*

At last, by a high stone wall, horse cropping wild mint
I took the roll of paper & added another song
To that of the crickets, the arrowflight of notes
A nightjar releases. Words like dawn-mist
Lifted off the pasture. The low Cevennes in the distance
Showed me how far I had to go
I sensed my heartbeat soften in the folds of land
That rolled beneath me. I was cupped
Within the hollow of my lady's hand

57

Love Poem for the Room

I have to invent the things we do
It's too big, you tell me. I love it
You always look thoughtful & ready to let go at the same time
I like to be able to see the clock & watch the hands move
We turn our faces away, as the curtain ripens with light
You grow from that tiny circlet like a dream

Then there's the moment when you hesitate
I wonder what wd happen if you called my bluff?
The only thing I have that I can give is what I get
I'm a missionary, addicted to the way you say yes

So to the moment when you skid off yr smile
I see that slight self-consciousness transformed
It's become something quite deliberate & unplanned
As you trample over me on all fours

Newton's Loft

Land of undelivered kisses,
Almost there's & near-misses
That's England on the map below
I'm parachuting down with Jill
'I hope,' she says. 'they didn't pack
Our canopies the first of April'

Whack!

The silken brakes take hold

Affinity's this slow descending
Graceful, mutual & friendly
Gravity is like a flower
The earth unfolds magnetic power
Shadows blossom from the sun
We drift together & become (the single) one

The Bastille

This is a prison of livid souls
Take off yr damned clothes
Feel yr nipple slide into my mouth
Between yr legs is a field of razed stubble
They have set light to you, burning you off
The smoke of yr scarred skin fills my nostrils

Behind the bolts of yr arms
I hear life-giving heartbeats
Someone is about to make a confession
What excites me
Is the drawn sword of yr satisfaction
Yr implacable witholding of basic supplies
The curved block of yr sex
The falling blade of yr sighs

Whoops, Wrong Bathroom

Androgynous creature in the shower
Dewy nipples of a just-pubescent girl
Adorable minxette, wearing no perfume
Except the tentative aroma of assent

It was likely others wd come
Sharing the water, using the foam
What wasn't ever the innocence
Of soaping one another's back
Became a definite conclusion

On the tensed tiles. The vocal gasps
That both held on to, not letting
Such admissions go, made one realise
How freedom first enjoys, then betrays itself
How voice sobs, confesses, & then lies

Robert Says

'Robert says you are a poet?' Ah, yes
Robert would say that, wouldn't he, whoever
Robert is? And now we know Robert says that
We're left speechless, not to say thoughtless
Altho her eyes are signalling the kind of interest
One might have for a member of the five-piece
Drainpipe Orchestra who play nightly at the Café Enterprise
'And what have you written?' Nothing madam
Except a few cursive doodles, the poetic equivalent
Of a defaced wall here & there, or a piano
Taken apart with a hatchet: Impromptu 34
'Oh how interesting!' And certainly there is interest
In the air. It resembles the emptiness of a complicated book
Perused, mused over & finally unintelligible

'And have you written any poems since you've been here?'
I haven't been here *long*
'Well, how long does it take you to write a poem?'
Five minutes, Madam. As long as it takes
You to abandon a flirtation & decide
This one's a weird-O. In fact, probably quicker
I am writing poems between our strained locutions
With my imaginary aerosol spray I've written
Sonnets all over yr sideboad. Yr decor is dishevelled
With terrible epithets. The hole in yr bit of the ozone layer
Madam, is wider. Tanks are moving under yr blouse. Yr tea-cup
Is about to undergo a molecular breakdown...

'I see...'

'Robert says yr poems are rather hard to understand.'

BOOK TWO

Muse

Well, & if the goddess came stumbling in
Kicked over the empties, joined me on the mattress
I know there'd be someone upstairs screaming
'Can't you control that girl of yrs?
But she'd make no noise. She'd be the soul,
                                    the heart of silence

So I lie here on this bed
Blessed with boredom, the energy of nothingness
And thrill to her non-existent kiss
I know she's waiting for me on a street corner
Hiking her skirt, smoking a cigarette...

And I know it's too cold out there. And foggy
And I'm too lazy to put on my coat & go
And she'll be waiting anyhow, sometime, somewhere
Like Truth in a Waiting Room, patient on a chair...

She

She is snake-beautiful
She sloughs the dress of fashion
She faces the discarded moment, smiling
She is accomplice to the accident of nothing

We must find her
We must wait for the shabby intruder, her guardian
And wrestle him down the steps, when he comes
The long straight steps that go all the way down

She waits for us to stand up, dust ourselves off
She has all the patience of disaster
She points to the limit of ourselves
She beckons us to follow

Reasons for grasping the angel
Reasons, but none of them are here

Yes

Watch me with yr grey eyes
Walk down the street as if you expected
Men to drag their tongues along the stones behind you
Keep the human movement going
Switch yr behind in those tight, scarlet pants
Prowl out along the branch of the afternoon
Ignore the herd of men breaking from pasture
Who throng the landscape as everything you are
Becomes the street. Speak to me quietly
As you sow yr body in that scattering, uphill walk
On the fertile darkness of men's sunglasses
Ignore the suburban stink of waiting, circling
Ignore the jostling by the wall, the shuddering
The stamping, the snorting... tell me the low-voiced truth

Feels Like It, Sometimes...

The middlemen
Are buffing the dull toenails of the priests
Beer bottles are thrown at the moon
Communion's little fallen grace notes...

The naked Muse
Raises her hands, places her palms to the wall
The boys queue up to take their turn
Taking root there, like wild beasts

They worship from the hip
At the altar of occasion
Know a ditty for a song to sing
Know a tune for the tune it is

A reprisal. An endless, jerking gesture
Why do women take forever to undress?

To Let

Where you are not going
The place arrived at speaks of
Striped wallpaper, a beat up payphone
Knowledge forbidding you the stairway
You have two seconds to panic
Before lowering yr bags in the hall

Animals peer over the balustrade
The half-open door reveals
Venomous visions of the veldt
Smell of lions & armchairs, a recent kill...
You begin to hyperventilate
Yr tongue hangs over the lip of yr suitcase
They're bringing you someone's head on a tray. Keep smiling...
It's too late

The Brain of the Tragedian

Sundays in bed with Rosalind, if not Rosalind,
Orlando...Tuesdays in love with Polonius
Mercutio on Wednesday, full of garage-philosophy
Back to his suburban admirers for the weekend
Indolent sofa-women, lampshade brutalists
Butterfly-bicep tattooists, with voices gasping & soft

He struggled to finish *Reality By Rights*
Knew it wd never be a hit. From the window
He saw his name on the wind-stripped paste-up
And it was like the tide, or the gulls off the pier
Larger than himself, whom he saw only
Thru the wrong end of a rainy sea-front telescope

In snack bars...very thin girls
Leaned their breasts into a lovely mope

Amours de Garage

Casanova at work on two maidenheads
Simultaneously thinks as he pacifies, attacks
That these two fourteen-year-olds, luckily encountered
Are his mother, his sister, his wife & his old Gran
And deserve the respect womanhood is owed
The more so for being in a long line of almost pregnant
Chips of himself from the old block. Nevertheless
Bons souvenirs! he thinks, upending one, while the other
Is encouraged to find her own way, like water down a hill...

What's a wolf to do with his wolf nature
If not cross candlelit rooms in his underhose
Take belief by the hand & turn it to squeals of alarm
Believe that in the giggles of resistance turning passive
There's a gap in dress & nature thru which only a wolf can spring?

Sepia

Those old photographs of an earlier twentieth century
Omnibuses, bowler hats & bicycles. What a betrayal!
The painter in his studio with three naked girls
Each one more beautiful than the cunning strokes
Of the artist's brush. And their employer
Standing beside a Hispano Suiza in beret & goggles:
A dust cloud on the narrowing roads of France

Francis Picabia. And there's Modigliani
César Vallejo's an indian from Progressville
And the patient question his expression puts:
'What have you done to me, Europe?'
That's Apollinaire & Kiki over there. There you have it:
The surrealists with coats on, *Café Rotonde*, 1916
A tram with no number blind at the end of an empty street

Alcohol

At yr servile service, this pen, yr servant
Subject only to the yawns of his subscribers
Wakes, puzzled, staring at the teethmarks in his cock
Opens letters from the Pope, written in lipstick
Backs car out of the driveway, forgets direction
Does the memory phone-in on the *'Who are you now?'* show

Drives to a river, writes a poem to the water nymph
Surprised, watches her surface from the polluted scum
Sees how she reclines upon the thirsty grass
Contemplates her green smile, the scaly glitter of her legs
Writes a belated sonnet to the joys of *Absinthe*
Catches light glinting from a bottle rolling down the bank
Kneels & arrests its motion, brings it to his lips
Holds the cool carafe to his temples, stares thru the glass

The Night I Got Hypnotised at the Pinprick Café

During the cabaret, a visiting magician
Showed off his cloak, gold stars
On a swirl of black. They sucked me in
Disinventing walls, windows, doors...

Admitted so easily to the temple of love
I ran my hands across the slumberous lovers
Who woke smilingly & offered me their mouths
Their thighs, the sleepy strength of their embrace...

Until they saw exactly who it was
Customers, you understand, do *not* like being interfered with
Smartly finger-snapped from my absorbing trance
I saw the diners laughing as they handed me the booby prize
A menu of all my discomfitures, soup-stained & dripping
A prayer-soaked epic of pretended nonchalance...

Music While You Walk

I'm just a natural whistler, one of those
Lip symphonisers, fifeing
An indian & his maiden down wild white water
With this off-key instrument of mine
I tootle sullen urban streets
Into deep romantic chasms

On a mirror lagoon, they drift, becalmed
I need a melody for the floor of a canoe
Oo la la. Such modulations. It's stupendous
How deeply tongue can moisten flutehole
As I make the diddly stops against
The onward rush of sexually lonely air
Piping imaginary blades of grass between my thumbs
Almost a great tune rising from the breaks

Poem Ending with a Title by Benjamin Péret

Without people there'd be no journeys
And without journeys there'd be no dreams
Without dreaming there'd be no poems
Without poems...*this rhetoric's a scream*...

What we have here is the natural inclination
Of the grammar to run away with the bone

And the mood of the poet
Contemplating the abrupt departure, versification...

He'd prefer right now to be lewd
With the barmaid, Sonya. *Write me a sonnet, love*

Life becoming like, & thus explicable...
Move like that

Words & embraces, sweetie...shouldn't they be inextricable?
Remove yr hat

In Wonderland

The naked were done with their nakedness
Maidens reversed themselves
I viewed things differently & grew smaller
Then I grew enormous & cd not get thru the door
'Who are you?' sd the caterpillar, disgruntled
It was not a philosophical question

'I know what I did this morning, but I
Was somebody else at the time. There were, I recall
A lot of disappearing men in swallow-tailed coats'
'Aha!' sd the caterpillar, 'so they *were* imported mushrooms...
And when the queen says, *'Off with their heads...!'*
I suppose you appreciate the sexual significance of that?'

'I'm not Alice,' I said. 'Then what's the difference'
Said the caterpillar, ' between a fiction & a hat?'

Museum Piece

Librarians are thin folk & horny
They eat the dog biscuits of insanity
And stamp out rebellions with their feet
They're good at imagining
What it feels like to be sat on
Take off yr spectacles & rub yr eyes
There's a locked room
In which they keep people like you alive
They push beasts from a chalk-pit under the door
And the phantoms of violent, self-lacerating couples
It's interesting to be in a place like this
Where the present is always overdue
And rows of tiny people dismember books
With desire's fingers, tearing obstinacy small

Sad Cases

Language of rain, of smoke blurring the damp haze
Where the wrecked autos, one on one, mimic the grin
Of ultimate standstill. Language of trees, of branches
Grooming the corrugated rooves of sheds, of greenness
Drawn to substance, to the physics of houses...
Language of open doors, of darkness on the sill

Language of lovers, dying thru the morning
Where the beds rattle beyond recall, & the toothbrushes
Crumble in the filthy cup. Language of stench
Of lewd romances, of cookery, of bodies struggling
To exhaust the ways there are to fry an egg
Of making makeshift shift, of tarnishing the city
Corroding it with endless, drenching kisses
Language of dark sentence from the rust of mouths

Writer's Block

Don't like not having a notebook
No notebook to put things down in
Nothing to be scribbled on, writing against the clock
With an audience waiting, staring at an empty stage
And me looking for the notebook
Curtain gone up & everything. How long will they wait?

Well, it's not me that's going to appear tonight
Somebody sweetfleshed & wordless, with a body
Like a naiad, will trip across the boards
Flexible as a bank note. Writing is dreaming after all
And what cd stir the imagination more
Than money? See how the audience shivers!
So full of anticipation! They'd probably feel
Utterly let down if I came on dressed as a notebook

Could Have Been Me...Actually...It Was

In those days I didn't go to weddings
The same was true of firework displays
Royal birthdays, any kind of parade
All those uninterruptable assembly-lines of something or other
At which the audience stares, a bit crazed
Twiddles its thumbs & feels rather fuddled...

I kept apart from ceremonial
From the easyspeak of grave behaviour
Asked one day to give a funeral address
I climbed nonchalantly into the coffin instead
And was sliding wittily into the furnace
(A deliberate case of blind identity)
When I opened my eyes & saw my error
Tried to sit up & banged my head

Identity Card
(a substitution portrait)

He was at least thirteen parsnips in height
His hair a delicate flamingo pink
He resembled Robin Hood's leaner & meaner brother
He wore an expression of total eclipse
His nose was a distillation of hops & sea air
He had a voice like *Une Saison en Enfer*
And was frequently heard to put the question: Is it love in the rectum?

Subsequently taking up residence in a graveyard
He founded a religion that consisted of asking questions
Such as: Is it love in this graveyard?
Naturally he was fingerprinted by the police
Who used a convenient tombstone as a blotter
And were surprised to read, when the ink had dried:

Empty this

Les Extrilistes

Down here in the minority, the wine tastes like buffalo freckles
We're stupefied students, always sending out for ink
Stains on the table go right thru the floorboards
Down to the cellar, & on to China
We need the attention of Neptune, the psychiatrist
He smokes dolphin-suicide cigars
And the busts of poets in his sodden library
Are wreathed with trails of octopus ink
Down we go in our confessional bathysphere, always down
We seek the death & resurrection of ourselves
A huge expression with whiskers clamps our porthole
We know what we have come to see, & now we've seen it
Like particles of anti-matter, we gaze up that black nostril
We'd quite like not to see it anymore, if that's OK with you

Thoughts on the Virus

I may have the new ailment from *The All*
Deep space malignancy, shuttling down
To take up residence in my bathroom mirror
Dizzy, if I see you behind me
I need the touch of yr faithhealing hands
Half-asleep you are, half doctor
Vaccinating me with the prick of yr skin
My personal antibody, handing back
Death's card with a refusing smile
Protecting me as I raise my head
Visibility, you whisper, is presence
Catching a glimpse of my face in the glass...

How did my jaw, my hands, get so big like this suddenly?
And before I know what I'm doing: SNAP!

Gospel Truth

Next door the mattress springs are creaking
Neighbours doing nicely on their own
Atomic desires, you moan
And bang a heartfelt shoe upon the wall

Sudden quite terrific lightning flash
The house goes brilliant with its photograph
Then goes dark again. You've glimpsed
The poems you papered all the house with

In the shockwave of the aftermath
You notice that the ceiling's leaking
You sag. A blinded, cunt-struck Paul...

The passion-freezing rain whacks the roof
Next door they're shouting *Vive le Roi!*
Yr bare knees kiss the lino of reproof...

The Time

Season of yellow sputum, missed cabs & recklessness
Of rain & reversed decisions, of Autumn maybe's
Season of money, of used pound notes, of dollars
Of damp exchange bureaux & sullen Asian ladies
Season of the windswept Bourse & men in hats
Of blowy river walks to the seat of reason
Season of sinking ships & voices thru a neighbour wall
A spattered pane, a tubercular gust, a slammed door...

Season of phone calls, of moralists with no heart
Of thieves hurling stolen goods into the Ark
Season of negatives, of yr careless hands
Of a body turning on the knife of a caress
Season of dreams, of things that didn't happen, did
The hard-edged lineaments of maladresse

Little Bitty Pretty One

She floats in & perches on yr chair
Where you sit gloomily, staring at
The great world of doing, making & becoming
And tweaks yr earlobes with her fingers

All my life till now, you tell her
And even now, you don't seem able...
Still,you keep trying, tho you've a suspicion
She loves you, she loves you not, probably

She gives yr ear another twist
You're the hedgehog of her life, it seems
Which is why she never takes her shoes off
Never gets really comfortable

Never stirs you with the spoon of her life
Never gives you the small sweet lump of her heart

The Candidate

I'm the sort who flunks tests
Crumpled shirt. Cuffs rolled. Green eye shade
Pen chasing pages, pursued by darkness
I've abandoned my candidature
To an open window & the life of chance
From the desert oasis of my lamp
I've plucked this ludic rigmarole. It seems to confirm
The re-routed camel train now stops elsewhere

I'm recapturing the glory of Fundamental Error
I'm remaking the Ur Mistake
I listen to wrongness beyond the room
Scribbling incoherent murmurs down. With abject care
I fail to remember the shaggy dog story of the world
I pin a new tail on that examiner's mutt

Hopscotch

And then, taking off her clothes, I saw Sheffield
Lovelier than statues or the approach to Kings Cross
Where nothing exists that has not been seen
Yet teems with what you cannot see
Beautiful termini that light
The impatient oil in my head's lamp

The city was inscribed with the word HELP
In such large letters you had to pace them out
To find out what they meant. And the chimneys
And the rooftops were exhilarating: rainy summits
It took eighty jumps to cross the map on one foot
Eighty back on the other
To see that I had written LOVE
On a place where neither chalk nor candour reached

Very Droll

Funny is when the shy girl
Suffers a heart attack in yr arms
Or when the cruise ship sinks
With all funny-hatted holidaymaking hands
Even funnier is the kind of physics
Whose properties involve the abolition of physics

Funny also is when the pilot of yr areoplane murmurs
'I think I must be dreaming'
And you look out of the window & see a three-masted schooner
Pirates order yr aircraft to stand-to
A boy eases himself lasciviously into yr lap
Gives you an ironic, tongue-in-the-mouth disintegration kiss
Yr hair stands on end. Nothing to worry about, he says
The plane is scrumpled in a giant brigand's fist

Gallery

'The Wanker Surprised By His Mother'
Decorously we shuffle past...
Just two straight lines & a splotch of purple
The title's more interesting than the ink

The masturbator carries on indefinitely
The point of parallel lines is, they don't meet
As for the purple, it represents a question:
What am I doing here? And why?

(Or is that purple patch his mother?) Actually
No one asked what *she* thought, did they?
Never thought what she was supposed to, anyway
I traipse thru it with both feet

And if the exit is where I think it is
Stand there and wait for me. And don't stop

Coincidence

This train will terminate at Russell Square, sd the driver
We have two signal failures approaching, namely
The first jolt, which you will all feel, like this
And the second jolt which you will also

A friend of mine felled himself at midnight
Walking, slightly drunk, in his starry garden
An unseen iron post & an idea struck him
As I abandoned public transport for my legs
Haring up the stairs at Russell Square
Whacked my foot on a steel-capped riser
And saw my toes fall off. I scrabbled about
Collecting them in a box, all precious ten
And brought them to our next meeting...
Each one was the size of the bump on his head

Obituary

Heraclitus had a low opinion of Pythagoras.
Too much learning is no help to understanding
And understanding in the process of being simple
Is difficult if you've not learned how –

In his sixtieth year, troubled with ague
Heraclitus lowered himself into a pile of manure
The warmth, he thought, wd draw out the humours
He came out stinking, & died

Understanding, let's say, has nothing to do
With being *right*. Being right is, almost invariably *wrong*
So this immersion in a filthy litter
(Weakened as he was from a diet of herbs)
Despite what the neighbours say, had a certain gravity of purpose
That calms the irritated seeker after truth

Eskimo

Fat to fat, fur to fur, squashed nose to lip
O for the igloo of that cold contentment!

>The youth dreamed of it. He was like a garment
>Found on a rag-pile, ripped –
>No skin within that wind-pitted coat
>No palms to warm the pocket's hollow
>No fingers groping from the cuffs, no throat
>Beating with blood against a filthy collar
>Trousers hoisted on a skinny column
>Their creases hung like knives along his shanks
>Nothing in his codpiece but a piece of cod, mmm…
>A jacksex kind the world of flesh outflanks

>>*Arms above his head, crouched low*
>>*A cornerless person, waiting for snow*

It Is Not Sufficient to Be Elsewhere in Order Not to Be Here

Something tells me I got this far
'You got this far,' it says, like a handshake
One of those lines that people like to draw
Holding a flag, a pistol or a watch

It bothers me this line, I keep moving it
Backwards & forwards in my mind, to arrange
My life better as one tidies up a room
So everything is easily to hand

But the lines turn to string, become a tangle
Mesh my ankles & trip me up
I keep lifting one leg & then the other
And the briar of entrapment rises to my waist

Suddenly I see myself as a natural growth
Rising from the idea of disaster like a goat

No Title

The ship of poems cracked apart
Yielded up its word-hoard to the waves
A secret vocabulary of people's hearts
No page had seen the printing of...

A dark slick blown by the wind
Leaked from the *amphorae* as they fell
Towards the deep... A concentrated darkness
That heaved & sank upon the swell...

It rinsed a shabby beach, where shuffling folk
In ripped raincoats & shapeless hats
Gathered the stuff gratefully into their arms
Thinking, at last, they'd make the difficult easy

Built a fire & stood around, their palms
Towards it, pleasantly watching it burn

Paint This One, Picasso

The picture was perfect: an open window
A tree with an abstract blue sky behind it
A tiny-headed pigeon sitting on the sky
No, not sky exactly...I am talking here
Of the tree's top. And grey-blue it was
With a white button for its head
Stupid, aimless, disgusting...& very high
All I cd hope for it to do: was fly

It did not. Picasso said once
Any friendship combines the possibilities of sex
I did not feel friendly toward this pigeon
Nor, indeed, toward Picasso. The tree wafted slightly
The bird was neither in nor out of the canvas
It just sat there, wobbling its brainless neck

Looking up, I caught a flurry of wings
In the top left hand corner of the frame
Two girls had been baring their breasts in the sun
And a dark youth of the country soon
Partook of this convenience to fondle one
Some brute starts to maul a pretty girl
Eh, Picasso...?
Fact is, *she* might be the brute

If this was a morality play, I was not the author
All had been observed from the corner of an eye
Reality seemed very mediocre, & its translation
Expensive even, beyond the need to fly
That Dada pigeon had given me a headache
I was left with my notebook & a cubist mistake

BOOK THREE

The Proving Ground

This is the alphabet
You can make words out of it
Words like *afraid* or *dark*
Phrases like *Have you finished?* & *Can I go now?*
I'm eating this alphabet. It's made of noodles
Words like *soothe* & *cunt*
I push them around with my knife & fork
And something emerges from beneath the sauce

I often wonder if spelling really exists
The ordinary kind, I mean, that wins prizes
And knows about *i* before *e* except after vanishing
And whether correct spelling tastes better
And if this golden blaze in my head I feel
When I eat the word *touchstone* is really haute cuisine?

Misprision

The cell I cannot get out of, freedom
Is too much like lateness or being too early
I'm a farmer with no harvest, nothing to do
But wait for someone to come, a bandit
To steal everything that has not ripened
Leaving the granary as empty as the sleeping golden head
Of this beautiful, lazy girl I dare not wake
Dare not tell her she is not here

Liberty is the bars on my window
The perch I sit on, jackdaw jailbird
Talking my ugly talk to the incessant clouds
Making a trapdoor in curious heaven
That were she here to tiptoe across
I cd so easily open it & plunge her down

Après Moi

I was queuing outside the Museum of Forms
Where beauty is portrayed as deluge
Where the marvellous is lashed to rooftops
Where time's buildings strain at their moorings
And the eager crowd is carried off
Clinging by its fingertips to uprooted images

I opened my mind in amazement at this
Fell into a violent, photogenic hole
A bottomless & disconnected falling
Along with telegraph poles, pillar boxes, street furniture
Like real life, I thought, as the lamps pinged on
Illuminating the city of our swept-awayness
And the rescue team winched us to safety with cries of 'Hold tight, mate!'
Smiling down at us from their crane, in bruised light

Tubtime

I sit naked on the side of my bath
Writing poems to the goddess
Clouds of abandonment come off the tiles
Scritch-scratch. Passionate notebooks

Outside on a window-cleaner's ladder
Leather is earning its keep – *scrawk-screek*
It'll never render that frosted pane transparent
So no one'll ever see me sitting here, like this

Venus is rising from the steam
She opens her heat-reddened arms, her lobstery breasts
Presents me her soaking hams, gives me a taste
Of the shuddery throat of her welcome

O foolish & impossible one
You don't do this for money either, do you?

How to Get There

These are the wrong instructions
For people who haven't got a car
To follow on foot, by bike, for whom
Memory is a twisted signpost
Goddamit, Agatha, which way now?
Until they buckle a wheel, or hole a shoe
Recollection coming true

These are the maps, the reconstructions
Of bosky tufts, roaring sea, the stiff
Of night falling on the pliant land
As, widdershins, a luminescent hand
Conjures up yr old lost love
Points toward the cliff
And gives you a terrific shove

Cave Drawing

Stendhal's sublime repugnance
'To speak of myself
Of the sum total of my shirts
Of the mishaps to my self-esteem...'

Bison flicker on a torchlit wall
Better to imagine the artist's crouch
The scrape of his tool, the stink of his pelt
Grunts in blackness, perfect sincerity

Talk best when no one is listening
Language blundered in out of the rain
If you have something to say, say it in the dark
No need to speak of shirts – let those tall-necked creatures
Browse the leaves of yr thought
Burping delicately into yr underclothes

Lip Service

I take off my clothes & lie down with my girl
Head to tail, finding her out with my mouth
Her thighs gently fold across my neck
Like rope

A small strong hand presses on my skull
And her legs tighten round me with each groan
Deeper & deeper, I lodge my tongue
In her name

Halfway there & yet I'm still here
This is what bothers me, this clinging
To people as a way of being nice to them
While I try to describe what it's like

Paused, pleasurably, over metaphor's trap
Feeling the shiver that soon will let me swing

Tools of the Trade

Arethusa turned into a well, her lover a stream
To flow more copiously into her
You can visit that bird-spattered trough on Sicily
A dismal swirl of feather-laden stains
How plentifully can a man flow into his poem?
An obdurate porosity existence has
It makes our poet think of drains

And other symbols. What use, after all
Are the stars and fleas in his unmade bed?
He stares, mumbling impertinently, out of the window
As morning's boat comes skimming over rooftops
And the rower himself, a giant black man
Naked to his toenails and covered with sweat
Hauls dawn behind him like a winding sheet

The Mounting Stair

Every day the ceremony is the same
Climbing the many floors to my room
That is under the eaves of afternoon
On a day of unexpected rain

The ceremony is done so publicly
That no one at all notices it
Like someone who does not walk or does not sit
The difference is performed invisibly

I hang out my Long Johns for those beneath
Message of damp leggings from the tiles of the roof
Gaze out across the city spires & towers
Hear the fat girl coming up those endless stairs
She hits each landing with a breathy '*Oof!*'
I prowl the room in underpants & teeth

Match

The game of love, we played it seriously
Laughing our heads off to keep from thinking
Just how serious it might be
If one of us ran out of the court, beyond the lines

Or lost the ball in sprawly undergrowth
Or had the racket simply snap in one's hand
And what we also knew was how the game
Attracted its silent spectator, notepad on knee, the third party

Whose pen flew across the paper like an electric hare
Pursued by greyhound fingers, whose eyebrows
Seemed to underline a disbelief, as we capered about
Thinking we'd reached the source of all hilarity & pleasure

Even as we played, we watched the watcher writing us
Scrupulously analysing how we might almost win

Palais de Leaves

The forest strikes up the band. Rustling all round us
Moon is the dance-floor out of which we grow
The single trunk of yr body, the sweep of yr branches
This is Hard Symphony Hall, a concerto for us
I spit on my hands to get a better grip
And hold you still against the vertical of me

I'm the patron saint of anti-dance
St David of the penny, St Michael of the knot
I'm the oak-loving labourer you picked up at the Roxy
I want to show you how I feel about standing
With nowhere else for you to look but up
I want to make yr world a sky, have you see
A comet plunging home to die
Above these night befallen trees

A Slowboat to China

The captain eats catfood at midnight
Whiskas is his preferred brand
He studies the charts of his late expedition
Wonders where it all went wrong

He found his way to the sovereign's kneecap
Set them all talking by conjuring an anti-world
The ships, the men & the money, he mumbled
His lips gone far beyond her kneecaps now

He takes the chart, tears it, folds it, tears it again
'*Madness to be right*,' he murmurs, scratching
In unlaced shirt, the sweat of faithlessness about him
He's master of a vessel that never rides or rests

Bootsteps of men on planking above him
The lanterns glimmer. He grins like hell

Twelfth Century Rag

Love was the sister of Imagination. Together
They moved into a small three bedroom semi, just north
Of Ancient Agony Road. Love made
The curtains, while Imagination kept watch on
The neighbours. They invited guests: Dalliance & Opportunity
Love did the cooking
While Imagination talked & sang & made gesture
Her pale hands peopled the house
With fantastic sorrows & the food went cold
The guests, feeling utterly neglected, got up & left
Good Sense, enraged by the stealth of this uproar
Comparing it to modern music, or the daubs on art gallery walls
Heaved a Molotov cocktail thru the window
Burnt the lot to a crisp

Kissacop
(for Roger & Margaret Garfitt)

I sit in my two-piece suit, picking my nose
My scuffed Oxfords rest on the opposing chair
I've shaved my head. I wear a crimson shirt
And a tiepin in the shape of a pistol, naturally
Pointed away from my heart. Somebody shouts my name
Do I know anything in the 4.30 at Kempton Park?
It's time to put the gear on, & drive downtown

Underneath I'm wearing white silk stockings
Secured by a rosette to my inner thighs
Today we have to question suspects
Below my nipples, I've drawn a shouting mouth
My loins murmur like a coop full of hens
There's a message in lipstick across my kidneys
Today's the day I'm gunna meet my lover

Those Friendly Fauna

A great problem of our society is bears
Smooth-haired, giant, sexually deviant bears
Listen to the cash register of their belief
Listen to the loudness of their speechless growls
They know you like the silence of policemen best
They cuff you, grinning, to the arrest of please
Pour fabulously easy monkey-nothing in yr ears

You loll before their promises like a dizzy girl
Don't let them steal yr sandwiches & drink yr beer
This is their garden. Didn't you read the notice?
Don't pose together while yr companion takes a snap
What makes you think a bear's a man?
Don't let a furry bicep slide around yr neck
As the shutter clicks, you'll feel it break yr back

Pistol Sonnet

It was so easy to love her patience
The way she stood by the lake with a pistol in her hand
Loading it gently & smiling
The ducks, too, with their benevolent, rounded, brainy, dumb
Strokable heads...well...imagine if you can a world
With no ducks in it. And there they were
Quacking to shore in feathered profusion, thinking
Those dropped shells were pellets of bread

She raised her head to look at me –
Her grey eyes foraging the beach & the trees
In case of witnesses. Her mouth drooped slightly
As it would when I bent to kiss her
'It's me, you or the ducks,' she said
I was landscape as she squeezed the trigger

Season

The young man's gaiety makes him forget himself
He want to introduce his friends to everything he knows
Slips naked out of bed & into carpet slippers
Ready for adventure. Then he remembers
Another appointment. His friends have left town
They kept sneezing, & complaining of the air
The sun is perfumed on the grass, & outside
Someone is whacking down a relative with a spade

He climbs back into bed taking disappointment with him
Hugging it to his chest like a lover, & stares upward
His heart is thudding against the ceiling to feel
In his own breast, his own arms, his sizzling brain
How Spring is a bedraggled flirt, a mere episode
An urchin in the street, taking his name in vain

Nearly There

Only a few pages left now
Like steps down a hall, or serial silences
One after the other, when
The conversation seems to be running dry

And everything not said seems more significant
Than what was. When that moment of
Transition happens, from
Busy talk to comfortable quietness

Is hard to say. Between a faltering recollection
And a kiss, perhaps? As you round
The next corner, half-remembering
Where you've come from, the street

Is lined with trees in full foliage
And people on benches, turning to watch

Same Again, Please

What use are symbols?
Mountains, stars or seas?
We'll never climb them, visit them, sail them...
Here are some hypotheses:

You know that Arethusa became a well
You know her lover became a stream
The longer to flow into her
An endless & orgasmic dream?

That girl upon the bed, now, see...?
Don't nudge her awake
Fix yr song up, use
A cunning punctuation, make

Bright-tailed comets cruise
Impassioned virgules thru her sleep

Negative

At the end of the road is a house of shadows
I walk towards it like a revenant
A grey pedestrian whose steps disclose
The half-resolving nature of my temperament
Afraid to glimpse the ghost that lingers
There upon the brink of clarity, making constant
Lens twists necessary
To throw her out of focus properly
And misalign the verticals of her nose

Nameless trees comb themselves on a hill
The wind bends them to my vacillating will
In a silver window-blank she holds her pose
As I draw near, looking steadily back at me
Thru the wry aperture of her fingers

Terminal

Missing the train, he slowed to a walk
His breath coming in gasps as the last wagon left
And turned to survey the emptiness the tail light left behind
After the curve had magisterially taken it

The great apse of the station was full of birds
Muttering & shifting on iron beams
He stared up into the warm, clucking chaos
There was no one in uniform of whom to enquire
Why the exit was a single arc of blackness

The arrivals & departures board had clicked to zero
If the clocks were moving too fast for ordinary time
Surely it was because no one in authority came to slow them down?
He wd just have to speed up & begin to run again
Far beyond what legs & heart cd do

From the Other Side

The man explained to his astonished listeners
He'd been dead a while. Then a tag
On his mortuary toe had twitched
They warmed him up. Three weeks he'd been in the freezer
Had he dreamt anything at all during this time?
O yes. The moon kept sailing up, as if
Into the dark blue theatre of his mind, & a toy boat
Crossed a wooden sea, with an elegant tabby
Strolling its planks, a pole on her shoulder
And a spotted handkerchief on the end
What was in the handkerchief? they asked
Two pictures of a woman. A bundle of letters...
And the cat...? The cat spoke fluent Hungarian –
A language he'd never bothered to learn

On the Waterfront

When you look at me with yr hooked nose
And yr lips painted like saracen daggers
I think of wild dancing in the shacks at the edge of town
Near the port where the silent cranes
Stand guard over ships, empty of wheat
Yr eyes are green as flutes, played in the entrance to the citadel
Yr teeth are like the little white fists of God

Yr hair is jet down to yr slender waist
From yr throat to yr breast a line takes me
A tramline thru the cobbles that ends in a circle
On a far quay, where people like you & me cling
In a rusting shelter against the dawn
Reading the graffiti we glimpse in the gaslight
The scratched declarations upon the walls

Quixotic

Into the night the poets rode
Like the chaff of time, the dust of sloth
Their knees whirring & their elbows braced
Their teeth clamped to handlebars, thumbs on bells
They were magnificent. Windmills tottered
And fell. Emperors waved from collapsing balconies
Beautiful women spat broken teeth
And showered them with ivory. It was a race against
The grotesque swelling that overtook everyone, but nevertheless
The elephantiasis also gripped them fast. Their limbs
Faltered & ceased to whirl. Their necks became unturnable
In great torsos of sludge their tiny hearts
Heaved against the hill of themselves. Very slowly
The abracadabra of poesy came to a STOP

The Inventor Speaks

I never know what I've thought till it's vanished
Slipped down the waste duct of my inattention
Just becoming graspable as it went
I invented happiness, truly I salted
That idea deep down in yr expectation
For a long time I patrolled the creaking dust of my house
On the edge of lamplit shadows, stealth itself
And finally, I caught the moment of its going

Some things never change. This is Paradise
Where I've lived since I went crazy
My house is built over a large hole
In which I've buried all my ideas. Ideas
Like how to make ideas from nothing. I bring you
The blank paper of my wisdom. And a pen

Turtle Beach

What a relief to think I shall not write this poem
The words will not slide up, dreadfully
Like that automated hoarding up on the promenade
Which alternates *Batman Forever* with *Smoking Can Damage Yr Health*
Dissolving one phrase into another
With such technophilous facility, a poet can only twitch

Will not write, therefore, of the ponderous turtles
Nudging topless beauties off their sandy towels
To sit complacently on thousand-year eggs
Remembering Hero & Leander with ancient brains

There are, unfortunately, no turtles to be written
Just ice cream men men, deckchair maidens, radio noise
No genial snouts in the water, paddling to the golden hatchery
No overlapping welcomers, crying out in the breeze

Shake Up in Araby

They let you have a magic whistle
When blown, it brings them back, wherever they are
You get three blasts & three denials
An instantaneously concluded state of return

Of course they don't admit having left you
They're having a good time in the desert
Imagine it: a camp of camelskin tents
Clear bright water with a hawk reflected there

They move in their see-thru robes from canopy to canopy
During the cool, morning hours, carrying dates & coffee
On small, intricately-beaten copper trays
Visiting no one. Not even the prince. Keeping busy

They squat before wind-flensed sheep skulls
Their beautiful naked bottoms flash in the sun

Tie Burn

I want the seed of my life to be borne away
Not to be a waiter at the table of myself
Easing this diffident finger round my collar
I don't want to serve the me who sits there like a customer
In the too-tight waistcoat of a hanging judge
I'll fog the mirrors of this café with one decisive breath
I'll concoct a puzzle to divert the clientele
And my sentence will nicely vanish into mist

With my index finger in the silver steam
I'll write a single word which will suspend me
Weightless as a doorman who lets the doors swing
At outcomings & ingoings, smiling cheerfully, vacuously even...

I'll have a cool breeze waft my dangling soul
Now...lean forward. Cut me free

Lift

Sometimes the writing is no more
Than a pentouch, a delicate dragonfly music
That captures the weird stealth of its own progress
Filling out a dull envelope of air

It's as if, after a vague accomplishment of risk
You felt retrospectively breathless & afraid
It's as if, after letting the world tilt inattentively sideways
It righted itself with an unimaginable jolt

So now I, who have not moved from this chair
Read backwards into the shape I hadn't then seen
Something I still don't quite understand –
Something whose mystery is obviously mysterious
Something like a balloon that tugs me away
As I hold on, half-disbelieving, one foot on the ground

Thalassa

With a notebook on my lap, I gazed thru the window
At the sunlight on the heaving green
The single dark fin of a submarine Leviathan
That cut the ocean's presence into three

Beauty, the beast & me, I thought
I watched it furrow up the shore
And glanced at her, across the room
Waiting for me to put the last full stop

Laying down my pen, I watched them disembark
Men from the belly of a wooden whale
The pages of my notebook riffled back
An urgent breeze came off the tide

They'd come for the partner in my illicit marriage
She eased herself off the couch, watching them arrive

Poetry

The poets used to decide when the battle was over
When enough matter was to hand for an epic
And it was time to still the clash of swords
They called a halt, relieving the warriors
Who were glad to know they'd done enough for today
No need to worry about winners or losers
The rhythm of sentence ruled again
Their minds moved in step with the words

Now the narcissistic whisperers drift
Toward the hopeless edge of melody
Poets stumble in the shafts of language
Feeling for the broken metre underfoot
Silence falls open, cut to the quick
Measure's stately, pagan jig lies tripped

Closing

The time is full of people
Who have nothing left to lose
What can they still be seeking
As eternity is slowly confirmed?

The duration rises like a ghost
A single figure, alone, crossing
The silent park, ringed with trees
Where the rusted fountains gather whispers

Sits hunched in the last deckchair
Emptying memory into the still pool
Where moonlight darkens the evening
As far off a throbbing thing halts –

A taxi-cab at the park's edge
A passenger, who stands & shades her eyes...

Wrap Up

Thus I became, in my own person, America
Till everything was like Hollywood, circa 1921
Black & white, not quite threaded on the sprocket
Going imperfectly thru the gate
So a silver strip zig-zagged from left to right
And the piano-player, drunk on cigar-smoke
Was unable to play for the lightning that jogged his elbow

That world was my world, an odour of beer
And sawdust & men in wide hats, chairs tipped back
And actresses removing their clamorous clothes
On a regular contract to undress three times a year
Thru a haze of cheroots that had never been censored
And the imagination was in in the hands of the uninitiated
Making up the story as they went along

Now I await the final moment
When, thru technical mishap, as always
The final frames jam & repeat themselves against the lamp
Causing a stain of melancholy to spread across the print
And light to pass transparently thru solid bodies
Reproducing an infinitely sweet & shaming surrender
As being's stuff is drenched in ambiguous radiance...

In very big letters *The End*
Is written just where you'd expect. She's leaning back
Over the leopardskin couch & a man in white gloves & a hat
Holds himself like a vast shadow above her
And they freeze till the film judders & jumps in again
Making the pair of them close, giving me such anguish
I terminate their climax with a wild switch

CANADA

A Trip to Canada

No doubt one reason why I distinctly remember gritting my teeth & saying to myself: 'Canada!' was an unconscious decision to impose the habit of metrical patterning on sabotage. The application of spontaneously written non-sequiturs to Shakespeare's lack of honour, for example.

I wouldn't say that I drifted off into a semi-hypnotic state of getting stuck. No, I was definitely awake, tho I do not, looking back, remember much about it. However, I had a sense of audience in my absence from what I was doing. It was not that I felt man is in a crisis, I merely wanted to organise a Mallarméan prison break.

By stressing the importance of invisible embraces, I thought it wd be possible to commercialise anarchy. Indeed, the concept of making large amounts of money was never entirely abandoned. I knew that in ancient times the Babylonians, in a struggle with nature, had constructed a view of the world which suggested there was not enough cash around, & that God had said: *Let the money appear.* I also knew, of course, that it never had, but refused to let this stop me. Life must be serious, I thought, if it is to make people stop.

Actually, as I had neglected to take a map, it soon became important to admit to myself that I was lost. Canada seemed a long way off, & I was still in Finchley. But what other justification for childhood can there be, I asked myself, than getting lost? It restores the critical truth of home.

As I looked around me, I saw that everything looked very dull, very similar, and somehow very strong, like a redolent but ignoble cheese. Such powerfulness of mediocrity shd not sound odd to British ears. *We want the generous impulse to act that which we imagine.* I had therefore a very clear idea of what was in my mind when I began to leave it out. Do these thoughts seem epiplexic? *A poet is a bird who sits in darkness & refuses to cheer its own solitude with horrid liberty rattles.* And why not? Don't tune into the calculating function of freedom is the basic point I'm trying to make here.

When I think about my girlfriend's underclothes, I observe her indifference to my desire to remove them until I have actually done so. What an amazingly ferocious sense of humour she has! Despite overweening odds, however, I have contrived to bring them to you, washed & neatly folded.

And very well aired.

Lonelyheart

If you are between the ages of nought & a hundred
If you can smile while being hanged
If you have weddings beneath yr eyes
If you will let me undo the buttonless room of yr overcoat
If you will admit me to the Protestant hospital of yr thighs
If you think we will ever have carnal knowledge of eternity
If the dixieland goose step of the volcano in yr midnight is feeling unusually
                                                      savage tonight
You are almost certainly the girl for me

And when in the darkness of nude zebras
We algebra each other with slap-brained tenderness
And thy numb sweetnesses decode my antelope crosswords with pasture
I shall unpack thy little radio with an aerial of prophesy
And fashion the little scissors of thy reception into fountains
I shall unfold the shadow-Bethlehems that lie around us
I shall raise my saddle to thy S bend & say

YES!

Sisters

With sisters you never know where you're going
Whether it's the one or the other, or this one, or that one there
Making love to one sister you're often surprised by the swing doors
Which propel you thru to the entertainment section in the basement
Where clouds break on the hourglass of enough
And she chuckles & says 'you can stop now'
With a familiar yet uniquely damaging odour of rented linoleum

I've eloped with sisters & wished myself free of them
Free of their white legs vanishing into teeth
Free of those fingers that remind you of parlour games
Free of that tingling entrance by symphonic policemen

Sometimes sisters greet you by kissing someone else
So the kitchen reeks of Bedouins
Sometimes they allow you to caress their sandal-like wombs, which have been
                                    worn down thru antiquity
And you feel like Tiberius wearing a groove in the flagstones on Capri while
                            they crucified old *head-on-one-side*
Sometimes they edge their lovely, stockinged limbs over the sill of yr dreams
And let you undress them, as if they were pleasure craft
If you capsize them
They bewitch you with their unpainted planks & upside down names
But listen to what the vile margarine of yr intelligence is telling you:
This is a nightingale trap that's not been oiled for years!

One sister is fond of bushes, the other adores trees
You never know which of them it is, tossing her sprightly head in yr brain
When you enquire who loves nature better
She gazes up at you from the grass like sky
Reason with her, you will obtain peculiar pronouns
'Mine!' 'Hers!' 'Not yours!' etc
Sisters are like truncheons of paradise
They are a metaphor by Isambard Brunel
They span the clever Tay, the disgusting Avon, the avuncular Lea, the slippery
                    Trent, the cunning Wye & the outrageous Firth of Forth
They tunnel under the sea
Sisters am I awake, am I dreaming, am I a brother?
I love the shamelessness of yr admiration for waiters who are learning to read
I love the sublime shyness of yr pale, hooked nose
I love the nip of yr invisibly sharp goodbyes
I love yr laughter like a peal of bells in frosty weather

I want yr blue eyes to seek mine across the lake of unhired rowing boats
As if nothing untoward had ever happened ever

Sheep

(for Neil Astley)

Every shoe is a shadow
And the shadows hobble about like poems
Poems you encounter in egg-cups at breakfast waiting for you to tap them
Tap-tap-tap, it reminds you of the little hammers of the crucifixion
So when the crucifixion rang me up & asked me to lunch
I lunched heartily on shoes, sheep-shadows, & nails
'Nails!' I said. 'Very good! But the shadows wd have tasted better without the
                        sheep.'
And the sheep came out of the kitchen in herds that cd no longer contain their
                        grief
Grief, which turned out to be the big bill religion had agreed to do the washing up
                        to meet
And meeting the washing up, you saw it was full of newspaper columnists &
                        murderers
Murderers, my little friends, shyly coming to the outstretched palm of my life
My life like a bus turning the corner before the driver has properly turned the
                        wheel
So that neither wheel, driver, corner, bus, or life
Look as if they'll make it...

101

Snake Spaghetti

The forest with its tall glades of sunlight stuffed with herbs & raisins
The international language of Hungarian gangsters
A tremendous revival of interest in going round in circles
The passionate alcoholism of fish
Those who paddle up the river Cocoa in lemonade canoes
The secret whistler who is not to be notified in the case of his own death
Shadowy departures from forgotten stations
The darkness of those whose train-timetables have faded in the sun
A hasty breakfast before being snatched from yr mother
The removal of hairdressers to places of safety
The girls in the grain-dryer catalogues who dream of other girls, who are alive
The bringers of rice-pudding to the children in the fields
The sweetness of those who have been measured for lawns

The mislaid scissors
The consequences
The life

To an Unborn Child Contemplating the View from a Womb

Miserable as a reader on a couch
Whom the punctuation leers at thru a window
You see how the bricks are taken down, one by one
And cleaned by the temple prostitutes

You may not communicate with these lovely girls
Who will lecture you on luckless chance
They'll fill the apertures in yr wall with mouths
And raise the temperature in yr longing for something to happen

Don't imagine things will improve slowly
Be agitated, yet remain calm. Don't foresee what comes next
Try not to entertain the idea of lying back on the sofa
While strings of pale sausages are pulled out of you, endlessly

As you grow up
You'll find yr relatives
Have played perverse tennis with you
The scoreboard will be encrusted in strange white fur

Defend yourself
There's a law for everything that concerns
The distance from the head to the floor
Get yourself a lawyer, a plane ticket, a submarine...anything...

A family is an ambulance disguised as a butcher's van
With a life-size cow on the roof. Narrowly
Decapitated by bridges, it
Moos with the homicidal tenderness of the proprietors

Listen to the tyre-screeching madness of the life-saving 'where to next?'
You have been born, my friend
You have toppled into maturity wearing a new suit
This is Pandemonium Hospital

Nobody has been here before except you

Shakespeare

You pair of windowless clogs
All my life I've been doing the solitary bus-ticket tango
And look what it's got me: You
Why do you have to stink in that vanished manner?

The umbrellas of yr blossom leak
I can hear yr hormones ticking
You're a bomb of raspberries
Who asked you to zigzag like that?

Down this end of the shop, you're marked
Ancient British Leapfrogs
O thee! O thou! Great pronoun
Of imminent disaster, push off!

What language do we need to speak
To find the correctly denominated supershelf in the undermarket?
Deaf article rainspeak
Overcoatless pilgrimtalk, that's what

Outside are my downpour friends
In queues that no one can join
None of yr soliloquies will do the trick
I've no hope of getting into the Vatican now

Kind Canada* give me a scholarship, please
Let me off the hook of this *blah blah blah*
I'll be off, then, to study Arctic throstles
In kissing company with the proletariat of warm sunshine's toes!

* A reference to the absent Goddess of imminent departure

Close Calls

The best poems this century
Have been written in a lighthouse with the power cut off
While the boats fandango in the yawn-tossed seas
And the sailors harvest their migraines
For everybody knows a lighthouse is never without power
It's the inspiration despair of every schoolboy for miles

Pencils, meanwhile, are like appletrees
Poetry has a scent & we can smell it, think the schoolboys
And they write it by scrumping
Stealing up behind Fifi La Roach with their padlocks undone
For schoolboys know there's a Holy War
Which is being conducted by semi-conscious debt morticians
Who have underwritten the priceless overdraft of poetry
With the abject clay nightingale of goloshes
The presence of which will make us turn up our fingernails & croak

Now these schoolboys are alchemists
They're gramophone pawnbrokers of epic short tidal waves
Going by their semi-detached houses, the upstairs room on the right
I see the beautiful linen of their eyebrows promising to be great
The way their feminine fingers drub the cheap paper with tough language
I see them in the distillery of anxiety, drinking its fiery thimbles
Tuned in to the cracked owls of immense turpitude
As they write the story of their own devilmaycare hacksaw irreproachability
Under the forehead, by the wasp, on the green bench, in the century's garden

The Castle

When I saw you sitting at breakfast
Humming 'All I Want Is A Band Of Gold'
Amidst the willow-pattern dowdiness of the Archbishop's rude pictures
I heard the whispers of intense anger
Other breakfasters were exchanging
Sentences like eggs smashed invisibly on shining foreheads
Little stains of melody dribbled
Gently down the gloom behind their ears

Our love was a castle
We were intelligent turrets
From whose joke-infested battlements
We peered out at the enemy
I heaved the gun-carriage into its THINKING position
Sent forth a blue flash of reminiscence
Into the pretty dell where yr best troops were
And a tall poplar of smoke grew from yr eyes

Underneath yr tablecloth you wore nothing
Air was the beach we saw from our clifftop walk
We watched the suicides hurl themselves amusingly off
You were all energy, all philophical prowess
I ate you with my heart & my head
Constantly in disputation with yr nakedness
We gave our landlady
The secret creeps

When, beneath my fanatical reader's hands
I found you under the blouse of yr distress
The tide slowly withdrew from yr long skirt
And an old woman sang: *'Christ, What Have They Done With The Flood!'*
The last time I saw you sitting there
All alone in the ruins, recalling huge Aristotelian fucks
I had that heart-sure sinkingness of feeling
The walls had been removed, stone by stone

The Most Comfortable Tree Stump in China

I enjoy housework
I like stripping the music off violins
I love removing pre-war newspaper from drawers to find the neatly-chopped
fingers of previous careful lady owners
Sometimes the ceiling leaks
I sprint into action with old canary-baskets, erecting a trapdoor of budgets to
finance the drips
Sweeping up accidents is delicious
I love the micro-surgery of brush & dustpan, collecting the infinitesimal
marbles of shrunken tribesmen who squatted the area in 1976
When I hear the words 'washing up', however
I creep to the parlour thinking how greasy Bishops are when they try to baptise me
Bed-making awaits
The fluffing-up, the piling on, the aft & abaft, the my end & yr end, the
pillow maltreatments, the mattress melancholias, the sheety balloons, the
blanket prizefights
When you've made it lie on it, sigh on it, die a little on it & (not just yet)
expire on it
Preferably in the arms of the vacuum cleaner
For she it is whose single arm has the versatility we can only dream of with
our mere two
She is the Air Ministry of sweet suction
She wafts you this way & that in delicious trills of shirt flautism
No sooner have you been vigorously wafted than famished millipedes arrive
And I, who have known every feint & ruse of the caterpillar
I, who have hung upside down beneath the ordinary days of the week
And wondered if it was worth it, or shd I just drop off?
Let me tell you
It's no fun watching a horde of *Lumpenproletariat* crawlies munching the tidiness
So slip into yr newtskin waisted shirt with ballet-parchment buttons
Put on yr sheeny gunmetal deadman jacket with the elephant-diaper pockets
Squeeze into yr macaw-beak trousers with the cobra-tongue seams
Don yr wide-brimmed negro-nightfall hat
Break into a slow-footed hornpipe
Crush the peanut shells on the floor, what do you care?
Do the housework later

The Good Ship Venus

Don't lean on the cenotaph unless you can spell it
You haven't packed the hydrangeas with the Gatling gun, I hope?
Too many bruises flew out of the opened grave & began to vaseline the
                                                                    moonstones
Trigger-desolation, I call it, but the Queen had her dogs out again
You cd feel that England was being reduced to an air mistress by the nephews
                                                          of royal jelly
Bees were conspiring to fossilise laundries
Oranges, born of skull onions, were being released into the oil
You can see how England attracts dryads in T-shirts
Even tho there are no T-shirts worth wearing in Leicestershire
England prefers the heartening presence of diaries to bolts of lightning
The soul of a nation which is being drowned by novelists can only open the
                                          coffin of its knickers to the sly
So let us keep diaries
They can survive on babies, fish & chips & mosquitoes, if they have to
And when the diaries have astronomical fits in public
Show them mice glue

Mice glue! Mice glue!
England sinks to its knees like a giraffe with no legs
Its keepers tenderly bring it morsels of piranha fish, wrapped in dentifrice leaves
Will it have children in captivity?
I don't think so
You can't run before you can listen to mortgage relief
England becomes ethereal
England varnishes Michaelmas with tunics
I can't hold on very long to this brainstorm of sealion televisions

I feel like a man who has been defenestrated by an unlubricated periscope

I feel like having a beer

Cheerio

Mouth with Its Teeth Firmly Clamped in the Hand That Feeds It, Refusing to Let Go

In the larder,
Where fish is the mouth of poetry
On a tin plate, cellar-coloured
There is something trying to say
'Gunk'

'Gunk' it says, like great poetry
Epic poetry, poetry with its head in a bag
Poetry feeling the Laureate's behind
Poetry fogging a pail of milk with dirt
On which a crow has tried to walk & sunk without trace
Leaving only its footprints on the cream

Nothing stirs in here except a flutter of cobwebs
All the great schools are represented here by cobwebs
All the meaningful discourse of the *Phantom Cobweb Quarterly*
A pinhead angel proclaims the cobweb of deconstructed doom
Here are the tiny shining cobwebs of the undergraduettes
And the universally immanent about-to-envelope-everything cobweb
But in every corner of this aerial basement
From which the flies have all buzzed off & the spiders shooed away
There is a very strong stink of fish
A cock-eyed fish, with a patch over one eye, & a slanting grin
Extruding a small quantity of fish vomit, & remarking determinedly
'Gunk'

Cumulative...

There is a sailboat of question marks fishing in the gulf
And the children disappear like cutlery
Stolen, perhaps, from the Hotel Splendide after the executions
When it is raining & there are no more poets left alive

Candles of Destiny

Of course I remember my childhood – don't you? –
On which my relatives played Handel's *Lumpengesang*
Whilst the blind men lined the route & stared
And an amputated marathon ran the other way

All over the house you cd hear gargling
As of one who suspects his throat of lying
Whilst the young women gave each other mutual support
In the form of axe blades that were soft & firm as foundation garments

The superb blind men loitered round the galaxy
They stuck their tongues out at the stars
A thunderous brood of baskets undid the dawn
My ends, alas, were crucified with means

The little ducats of common speech ran thru my fingers
My soul had failed to harden properly
Felicity! Felicity! it cried, as
Powerful muscles of leafmould heaved at the door

I peered down the long wobbly roll
Where blank-eyed dice make bone meal of everything
With a throw & a curse & a fingersnap
I let my astral portion go

Then it was midnight & the snails
The cheap, mooching snails appeared
Weakening the flagstones with high frequency felching
And trying to look like kettles

Wd I not be awakened by a smell?
A smell of antique shop-pyjamas & elderly brides?
The odour of mourners cheering the alimony of tomorrow
When silence breaks like a fart across the stadium?

Drift, I say, drift on the incunabula
Let fumes release the aspirins of briar
Let stones unpick the raving beards of Cirencester
Let envelopes distil the telephones of fire

Acrobat Johnson

Whenever the shoes of the feet that belong to the girl in concete
Shyly approach the tiredness & ask for help
On the windswept corner of nowhere. This is the moment
Acrobat Johnson appears

When she slips into something more subtle
Like the sacredness of revenge
When she gets that 'fresh-basket-of-mackerel' feeling
Acrobat Johnson considers

And when the highest wire in the world begins to shake
And she walks down liberty lane in the air
And thousands of upturned mouths underwrite her progress with noughts
Acrobat Johnson trembles

She's only fourteen, his Nancy. Has
Gone with Billy the Kid & Jesus of Nazareth. She pleases
Carpets by laying the tummy of the mystery upon them, while
Acrobat Johnson disrobes

And romance is consummated on the great pile of literature. O great
Moments from the past
That are echoed by children in need of the present, above whom
Acrobat Johnson soars!

Are there moon-bumps on yr anonymity?
Is there a wilful tempest of vacuums in yr soul?
Do faith-disposal experts knock steadfastly at yr door?
Acrobat Johnson nods

To meet the fantastic tenderness
You must donate some tongue & some hair
Dial the Lyrical Anarchy Helpline, & rest assured
Acrobat Johnson will be there

Redman

You wd not go home with a sailor
If I had waited for you
With my arrow-quiver clunking thru the night
Where the black cat gorges on regret, wd you?
What did the rain matter, when the whoop of my prayers rusted to a standstill?
You danced, I knew, under the heating engineers
Under the taxi driver & the railway porter
You knew I was following yr caravan
But still you surrendered the charms of darkness
To the epigrams of equipment
Please don't go home with a white man again, my darling
Think of me up here on a ridge, on my pony
Looking for the enemy in the foothills
It's you I feel breathing against my smoke signal
That soft semiotic puff with which I repair
The holes in the clouds of my bluff
I can ride this horse clinging to his belly
But it's the invisible cavalry of otherness I'm afraid of
They hang on yr lips as I do to this grassblade
And my grassblade will never be more than one Chieftain at a time
The tribe is moaning & trying to summon dandruff answers
With ululations that echo my insect self
Little Raindrop they call me
Except when they call me Big Raindrop
And I beat my chest & drink gallons of firewater
And then they call me Big Fierce Hair Tonic
But still you ignore me
Even were I to become Tidal Wave Raindrop
I think you'd ignore me
I think I shall become
Universal Drought

Little Motor Moan

When I gull yr belly into farcical convolutions & pearl
                              with the monstrous depletions of nocturnal tantrums
I open my clenched eyes on yr youthful scabbard
And see how the absorbing monotony of yr punch & judy breasts
Is nothing more than a float of daughterly sighs that goes round electrical
                                        corners with the quietness of milk
Yogurt is thy name, thy face is ships, thy paraphernalia snapdragons, thy
                              storm sheets more bestial than lizards
I feel the thunder of yr admonitions crush against my bones like *force majeure*

When I see yr face in water, looking up at me from a bucket & with difficulty
                    place my erect penis over it as in a child's game of bite the apple
When I lift yr slopping heaviness toward the tabletop & spread yr damson
                                        thighs for my easy fingers
And the gibbering sandwich-leap of yr happy tongue wafts me into
                                        the yonder of hello
The *told-you-so*'s of my imagination are impaled on lacustrine toothpicks
Mules of destiny come galloping into view

This is the moment the entire 20th century goes lime buffalo lurid with test tubes
Its marshals & sheriffs, its ogres & cyclists
Slide cautiously over the hilltop in a curious parade (with banners)
To where we lie in the dandelions, throbbing like babies
After the usual misplacements of justice have been scientifically verified
And all the nibbles on our skin stand up like weasels
Sniffing the air as if we had breached the theory of goodbye
Like pieces of towel that nomads apply to swim in
Or a casket of poems happily excluded from the canon
Engulfed, arrested, mollified, &
Urinating gentle floods of the most golden flowery sententiousness
                                        into each other's mouths

Muffled Cries from Beneath the Eiderdown

In order to preserve
Yr glorious Nakedness in my sieve-like memory
I have had the alphabet privatised, & have myself obtained
Exclusive rights to the letter N

I shall advertise the glorious mole of yr altogetherness
By having a spaceship tow a banner round the earth
With the letter N prominently displayed upon it
(It's what we space people call a Nologram)

And it will orbit the beautiful polluted ball of *Terra*
(Shrouded in ejaculatory mists of steam & plaster)
And release a homely song of the uttermost *déshabille*
Into the radiant furniture of bushwhacked stars

Hello

(after Benjamin Péret)

My Spitfire in flames my castle flooded with Rhine wine
My ghetto of Spanish glances my crystal ear
My boulder hurrying down the cliff to flatten the local police
My milky snail my breezy mosquito
My bird-of-paradise quilt my hair of black spray
My exploded tomb my rain of red grasshoppers
My levitating island my aquamarine grape
My cautious yet mad car smash my brutal herbaceous border
My pissabed wombapple of my eye
My tulip bulb in the skull
My gazelle lost in a West End cinema
My tape-recording of sunshine my volcanic fruit
My hidden pond laughter in which lame-hearted prophets drown themselves
My tidal wave of blackcurrant juice my mushroom butterfly
My blue Niagara of unresting Spring
My coral revolver my mouthwell into which I stare
Glittering
Frozen as the mirror in which you contemplate the escape of yr hummingbird gaze
Lost in a white exhibition framed by corpses
I love you

Revolution This Time, OK?

No measles were seen yesterday loading tanks into balloons
At the corner of Lamb's Conduit Street & Wolfbane Close
But some strident angers fell off their balconies gesticulating
When the reader had finished testing his sandals on the ice
And there was a considerable amount of water in the battleship
Which had been navigating Trafalgar Square on a skateboard
Its anxious ratings peered over buses & royalty
For any sign of Villeneuve coming up smartly out of Whitehall
And a large number of pink uniformed sanctity policemen
(Known as Burkes, after Sir Edmund Burke)
Tried to pour a little Irish common sense into the tapwater
So the populace wd be mollified & go back to Cork
Where everything is stopped & an uneasy peace settles over the waves
Like three nuns pushing a wheelbarrow in which the pontiff is hid
Or a barefoot contessa gliding over the dew in her pyjamas
Crooning a little song of *Hardy, the Intrepid Foxhunter*
As the tide rolls in upon the empty & fathomless sand dunes
Where a single British tourist floats face down smiling at the fish
With a flag up his afternoon

Cromarty, Finisterre & Shannon

A book of poems is like a well without a bucket
The noise of falling it made reminded me of the absence
So I took a lift to the 23rd floor
And stared at Mephistopheles doing a bit of hang gliding
In the updraught from a baker's chimney
Until the absence tapped me on the shoulder & said:
'Why don't you arrest this Montgolfier motion
With a display of carols or something?'

I rushed down the stairs gibbering Koranic prayers
And sought the cool lavatory of contemplation
Under the urine-stained lime tree near the station
Where they sell spicy meat in Turkish leaf-pastry dusted with trees
And the women wear tall white hats
And glide over the earth like plumbing
And the absence leaned over from an adjacent table & said:

'A book of poems is a blackbird with paranoia
It's a passion for bellpushes
It's a loathing for raindrops
It's a yearning for explosions
It's a trembling for blonde
It's a raging for biscuits
It's a smarting for cheese'

Hmm

I felt like a poet on an operating table
I cd feel the rubber-gloved hands of the doctor rummaging in my entrails
Someone said: 'Scissors, Nurse Tweezedale!
Who is this patient? Is it Dr Jung again?
Give him the oxy-acetylene, will you?
If he gives us any of that
Collective unconscious stuff again
Cut off his ears...'

So I rose up off the operating table
With my guts trailing on the floor
And skipped round the room
Using my intestines for rope
Was I not a free man etc?
And the absence whispered:
'Plainsy plainsy marmalade
O U T spells OUT!'

Midget Killer

My neighbours have smuggled forests out of my sleep
Each of them earns money. And this money –
It's buried in my garden & the police, who are fully-manned
Look at me accusingly as if I had buried my shit alive

You don't mind being a monkey, son, do you? they say
It's time for me to climb a pole they have erected
I am extremely anxious to help them in any way I can
So up I go. There's a wonderful view from here

Keep going, they yell at me
When I reach the clouds, they are full of naked women
Who rather notoriously cease chatting when I arrive
The silence becomes awkward until it is broken by bees

I have a sense that people are trying
To hold a candle to the elbow-grease, before it fizzles out
They've all been thrown out of work by desire
Which clogs the machinery into which they've dropped it

I go round the women, trying to appear piquant
I take on the aspect of an interesting monastery
Whose gardens are planted with the ascending bean
That I, thru elegant polygamy, have reached the summit of

We need to accustom ourselves at last, I say
To the dartboard stockings of truth, the fishnet of ambulances
To the grunt-sized slices of bed leather we will need
If we are ever to get thru this gumption without feeling queer

And there is light applause, like rain
Which sweeps thru the landscape & then goes out onto the balcony
And can be heard coughing, from a distance
And complaining that the view of Lake Geneva is actually Barking Creek

Canada*

This is my dream country, it's full of people saying: 'Loggo!'
And the correct response to this is: 'Loggo to you too!'
It's wonderful how the arrows of convention fly to their targets
As if aimed by bachelors with lawnmowers in their brains
Everything is immediately ice-cool & French, with a certain amount of English
negligence pinned to the dartboard
A moose puts its head round the door & says: 'America!'
To which there is universal jeering, as of lighthouse keepers dancing the
Trans-Canadian Ambulance Foxtrot
As for the girls! the girls? well, the Canadian girls...
Just to see a Canadian girl is to contemplate religion
As if you had never contemplated it before, anyway not quite with such a *bears-
in-the-woods-are-my-friends-but-keep-running* sort of feeling
A typical Canadian girl has a nose like a pigeon, a mouth like an eel, a jaw like
a silk ear, hair like cognac, eyes like a hockey game, breasts like mother,
a waist like General Wolfe, thighs like tennis spectators & a voice like
parliament
It can over-pedal the tubes of a young man's harp, I can tell you
You tremble to kiss her & when you do you are almost immediately given a flag
It's a wholly new kind of bliss to be Canadian
First of all you get a flag, then you get a wife & after that you are allowed to
meet yr wife's friends' husbands
Canadian husbands are the lumber-jacks of tomorrow
They knock down entire forests of it with a ninepin swipe of their axe
Then they rest on their hatchets & wonder what happened to today
If their activities were laid end to end they wd resemble the Yukon, which is a
wild part of Canada wives are not admitted to
In fact, the country is variously segregated according to height, weight & wives
There are shopping malls, newspapers, & a large number of small boys
The latter travel the length of the country composing unicycle troubadour music
on quaint indigenous instruments carved from chamber pots
And in almost every town there is a gangster who will steal yr tower
But it's not necessary to take yr tower to Canada as there are plenty of wooden
boxes lying around on which you may step up to gain height
You can see the magic of incomprehensible emptiness from there
Then you will be given the wine of the country, which is electric-yellow streaked
with green & shd be drunk swiftly or not at all
Canadians have wonderful manners, they stand to attention when it rains
If they hear cannon, they erect subterfuges
When the poultry migrate, Canadians gather on hilltops & record the number
of eggs falling from the sky

* Kwaqiutl word meaning *exit*

119

Canadian cities are almost monotonously wonderful
It is possible to speak 20 languages & still feel aphasic in Canada
Each little bar has its own drink, its curious stools, its quaint yet commodious
cash-register
And the liquor consumed there flows majestically into the St Lawrence killing
the sheep
Canadians never laugh, except to show they are amused
They are courageous, inventive, toffee-nosed, apoplectic, imaginative, boisterous,
and dull
Every Canadian will treat you like a brother until the situation is explained to him
If mounties lean from their steeds & pat you on the head
And murmur in moustachioed voices: 'Deirdre Fool! Deirdre Fool!'
And chuckle tenderly, do not pull out yr gun, this is quite normal
O normality, dearest & least understood apparition from the vegetable kingdom
How often have I held that fragrant herb to my nose, climbing into bed with my
invisible Canadian maiden, thinking of stout legs & rucksacks
How often have my visions been assaulted by redcoats with queens in their tunics
As I grasp my pillow & dream maple syrup chipmunks
Hearing she who digs holes with her mechanical elbows say softly:
'Loggo!'

DEUCE

Tennis Anyone?

(for Matthias Adelhoefer)

Above us all: a tennis player.
A sport in shorts.

He beckons us into the changing room,
where the boys shout 'Steve!'

But our name's not Steve. It's not even Arthur.
Names are meaningless here.

In tennis the word 'love'
equals zero.

We crouch on a rectangle of nothingness
with a bat of apertures,

looking at a net put out to dry
across which dead flying fish do not take off.

We have to fail to respond to this provocation
by crying: 'Not me!'

A clerk
from the sepulchre of weights

& measures
intones the emptied word.

If only he cd be persuaded
to say (instead of 'love')

'Steve is expressing a need for warmth & closeness.'
Or 'Arthur, slim, 40, with a vertical right arm

wd like to meet Frenchwoman or similar,
view bobbing apart at a distance & waving & shouting.'

It cannot happen. We are wind-borne seed.
The world is an airy bag of white lines

in which we make sweeping gestures that are not
actual blows. Our priests employ

words like *Love. Advantage. All.*
They do not mean this.

Even less do the principles they serve
uphold anything. Rules are made to bounce.

And no one cares about the fish. How it feels, for example,
when someone hauls you out of yr element

& in blank contradiction of the fact
that you are not spherical

whacks you at a reticulation
whose nine billion holes fail to let you thru,

confirming the name a cleric in a high chair has just denied you
by shouting: 'No ball!'

Our chests are water. No wonder
our hearts bump & go under

like stones that fail to skim.
And each time the swivel-necked mob

wishes to kiss its neighbour,
& the neighbour turns away its cheek

or the umpire cries: 'Love all!'
blindly we dive,

snagging the nets,
the rackets, the lines,

bearing them downward, comet-tailed,
in finny cadences

thru bars
of marine sunlight,

to scribble
fierce cacography

upon
the vellum of the mud.

Midsummer Night

Deerskin dents the earth.
Over the dry-leafed ground
easily, a redman lopes
along the twig-infested path.

Someone's footprints
wait to be tried on for size.
He sidesteps them
& a soft coo-chirr of surprise

rakes the back of his throat.
He's come for the masque,
played out for lovers in
the presence of the king.

He can hear a virginal,
see the pomaded & powdered pair,
arching their wrists & elbows,
warm flesh, pink tongue, his girl.

The helicopter chatters overhead.
A psychotic indian is on
the loose from the institution.
A man who touches the dead

with his fingertips
to cure them, who babbles
of daylight's frailty. The chopper
pilot grins at the reports.

Fanblades drive the trees
this way & that. Small figures
in the pantomime below
motion him to leave.

The sergeant slips a brainpill
in his mouth. Two a day, he takes
against the something in his skull
that wants to grab control.

Down there, two actorly hands made
dark by flounced white wrist-ruffs,
push wide the woman's thighs.
Under whirling blades,

the cloud-cop thinks kiss kiss,
wondering who the public is,
& why they drive their jeeps across
a lot of nowhere for a show like this.

He swings his craft away
to quarter other sections
of the forest. As the rotors
slowly fade, dispassionately,

the king begins to bless
the marriage. The listeners hear
ghostly steps of words
that walk in front of sense,

unaware of how around
this queer theatricality,
a skinny chieftain skirts them
in tight & tighter circles.

The slap of moccasins
brings back a memory
from a dream periphery
they had not thought existed.

What they feel, they ascribe
to scandalous excitement –
desire's enactment
upon a woman from another tribe.

The night is thicker.
With shining fingers, the courtier
undoes her collar.
The music snickers

And in a drunken
wasp-machine, rudder gone,
his vaneship lurching
like a seasick galleon,

the pilot aborts his patrol.
He feels it spreading upward like a chill,
the dark that fattens far below.
He swerves from hill to hill,

tries to hold a line.
As midnight strikes,
the last one of his tribe
completes a field of force

around the weird arena.
Backward bolts of lightning
undo the nerves of everything,
a glare so bright

it pushes eyes wide...
But cannot remedy
the pall, or stop the comedy...
The dead push thru the soil.